Science F

THE SALTERS' APPROACH

3

Looking into Science

HEINEMANN
EDUCATIONAL

FOR THE STUDENT

This book continues your course *Science Focus: The Salters' Approach*. In this course you are encouraged to think about the world you live in and to use scientific ideas and investigations to find out more about it.

When you heat a solid to a high enough temperature it melts.

When you heat a liquid to a high enough temperature it boils.

The pictures and parts printed like this set the scene for the activities you will carry out.

Information you will need is given in boxes like this.

Tasks for you to do are indicated like this and questions for you to answer are numbered.

This book will help you to use scientific ideas to find out about some things which happen in people's everyday lives. We hope you enjoy doing this. We also hope that it will encourage you to think about things in your own life which studying science might help you to understand.

The Salters' Team

CONTENTS

GREEN MACHINE

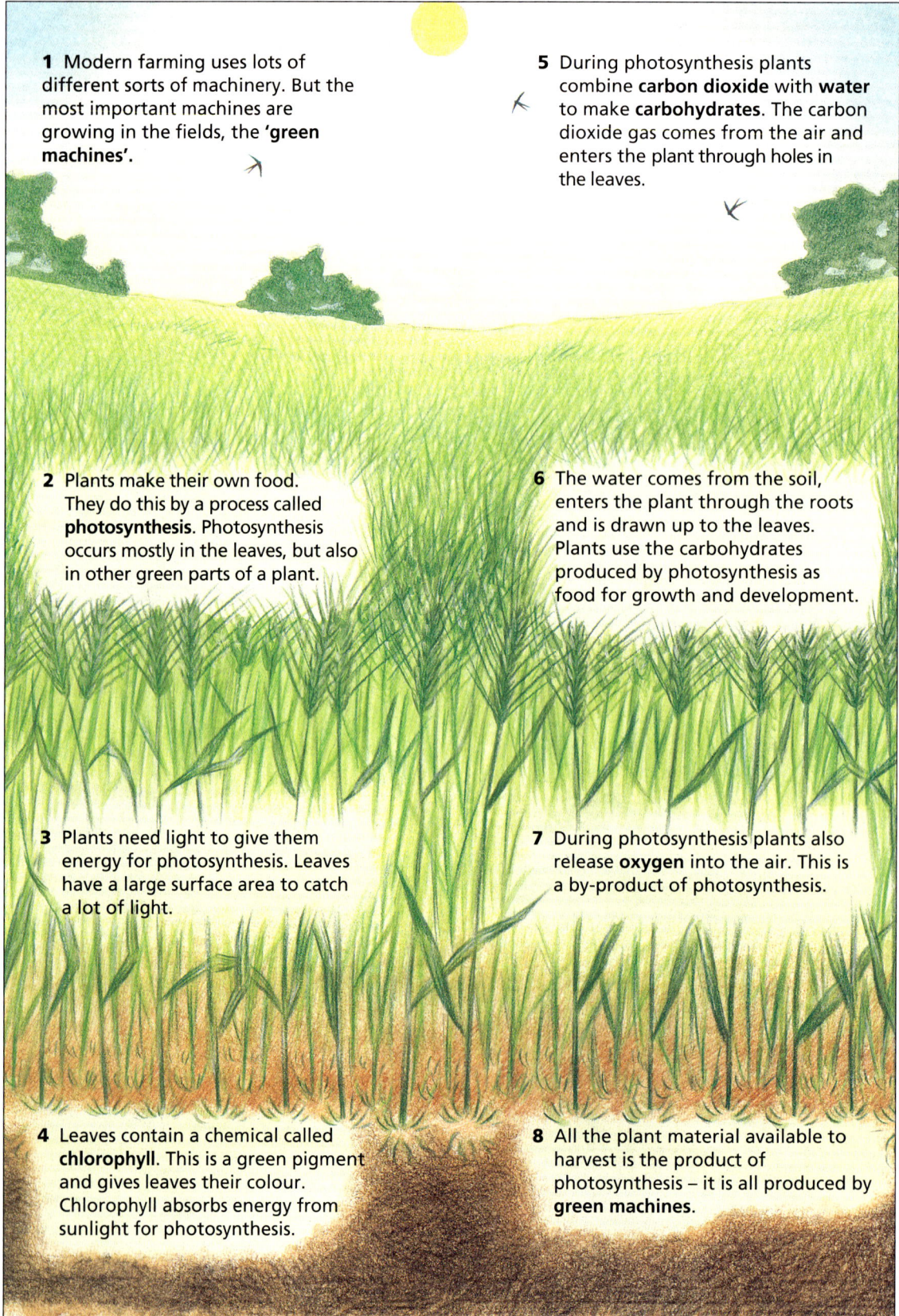

1 Modern farming uses lots of different sorts of machinery. But the most important machines are growing in the fields, the **'green machines'**.

2 Plants make their own food. They do this by a process called **photosynthesis**. Photosynthesis occurs mostly in the leaves, but also in other green parts of a plant.

3 Plants need light to give them energy for photosynthesis. Leaves have a large surface area to catch a lot of light.

4 Leaves contain a chemical called **chlorophyll**. This is a green pigment and gives leaves their colour. Chlorophyll absorbs energy from sunlight for photosynthesis.

5 During photosynthesis plants combine **carbon dioxide** with **water** to make **carbohydrates**. The carbon dioxide gas comes from the air and enters the plant through holes in the leaves.

6 The water comes from the soil, enters the plant through the roots and is drawn up to the leaves. Plants use the carbohydrates produced by photosynthesis as food for growth and development.

7 During photosynthesis plants also release **oxygen** into the air. This is a by-product of photosynthesis.

8 All the plant material available to harvest is the product of photosynthesis – it is all produced by **green machines**.

◣ Photosynthesis

Use the information on the opposite page to help you with the following activities and questions.

▪ List the starting materials for photosynthesis.

▪ List the products of photosynthesis.

▪ Write a word equation to summarize the process of photosynthesis.

1 Where do plants get the energy required to carry out photosynthesis?

▪ Explain why chlorophyll is important to photosynthesis.

2 If green plants did not photosynthesize, what would happen to:

● the amount of oxygen in the atmosphere

● the amount of carbon dioxide in the atmosphere

● our food supply?

◣ Food for plants and animals

Plants make their own food by photosynthesis. We use food made by plants as food for ourselves. We either eat plant material, or feed it to animals and eat animal products. A large variety of plants are grown as food for humans or for animals.

◣ Wheat

Directly or indirectly, plants provide all our food by photosynthesis. One of the most important food plants is wheat.
The pictures here show different stages in the production of bread from wheat.

▪ Write a sentence explaining what is happening in each picture.

▪ Draw a flow diagram to show how bread is made from wheat.

FEED THE WORLD

Growing more grain

*Grain provides about half the food for the world's population.
Until the mid 1980s grain production steadily increased. In 1950 world grain
production was 700 million tonnes. In 1986 it was 1.8 billion tonnes.
Distributed evenly, the world harvest of 1986 could have fed more people
than the total world population.
The improved yields were achieved by:*

- *planting new varieties*
- *using fertilizers*
- *applying pesticides*
- *irrigation.*

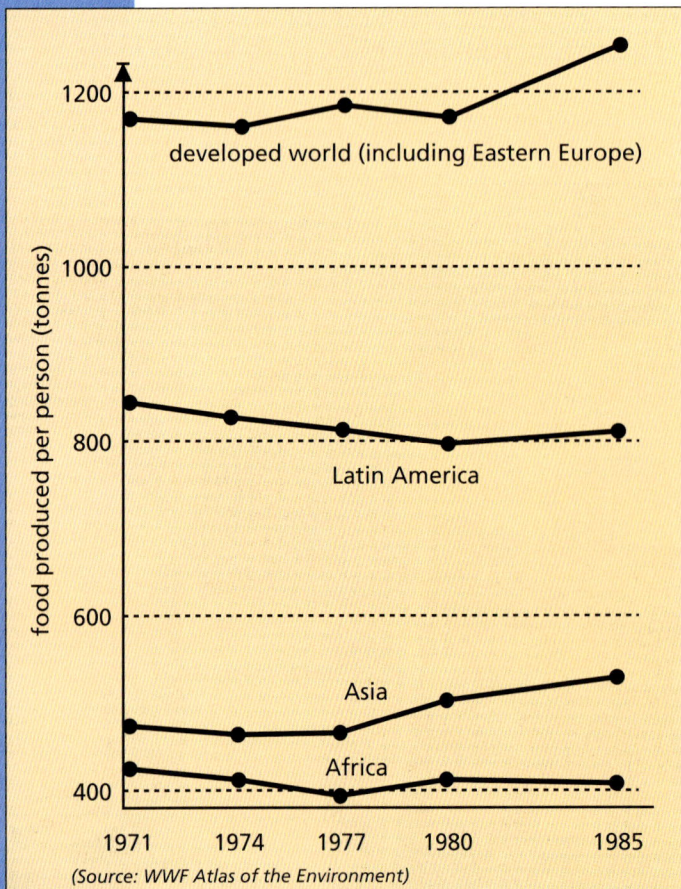

developed world (including Eastern Europe)

Latin America

Asia

Africa

food produced per person (tonnes)

1200 — 1000 — 800 — 600 — 400

1971   1974   1977   1980   1985

(Source: WWF Atlas of the Environment)

Is it enough?

*Farming practices have improved all over the
world. In some developing countries, food
production has increased, but not quickly
enough to keep pace with population growth.
Africa now produces 27% less food per person
than it did in 1967.*

Look at the graphs opposite which show
the amount of food produced per person in
different areas of the world.

1 Which areas of the world have the highest
food production per person?

2 Which areas of the world have the lowest
food production per person?

Suggest some reasons for the large
differences in food production per person
in different areas.

Between 1980 and 1985 the food
production per person rose in the
developed world while in Africa it dropped.
Suggest a reason for this.

Producing less grain

After four decades in which world grain production increased, the total world grain harvest of 1987 fell back to the level of the mid 1970s.

Grain production grew from 246 kg per person in 1950 to 345 kg per person in 1984, but dropped to 296 kg per person in 1988.

In 1988, for the first time ever, the USA produced less grain than it needed to feed its own people.

1989 was the third year when not enough grain was produced to satisfy world demand. World grain stocks fell and prices rose.

Bad weather was one cause of the poor world harvests. India had a drought in 1987, and the USA, Canada and China had droughts in 1988. The conditions were too dry in these major grain growing areas for grains to develop to their full size.

Two other factors are thought to have influenced global harvests in 1989. One factor was air pollution.

3 How do you think air pollution might affect photosynthesis and thus crop production?

Another factor thought to have resulted in lower grain production was poor soil quality.

4 How might a drop in soil quality affect the growth of crop plants and lead to a poor harvest?

Food and hunger

Over a billion people do not get enough food to enable them to lead fully active lives. This is about one person in every five in the world. Obviously, just increasing food production per person is not the solution. The food must get to the people who need it.

Collect newspaper cuttings or make notes about television programmes which give reasons why so many people do not get enough food.

Discuss these questions:

● Do you think it is better to send food from developed to developing countries, or to help developing countries grow their own food? Explain your answer.

● What difficulties do you see in carrying out your preferred course of action?

GENE CONTROL

Breeding better plants

To enable food crops to be grown in countries where the conditions are not ideal, we need to breed plants which:
- *can withstand adverse weather conditions*
- *are resistant to disease*
- *are easy to harvest*
- *give a high yield of nutrient-rich food.*

To achieve this, we need to understand how plants grow and reproduce, and how the features of one plant can be passed on to another.

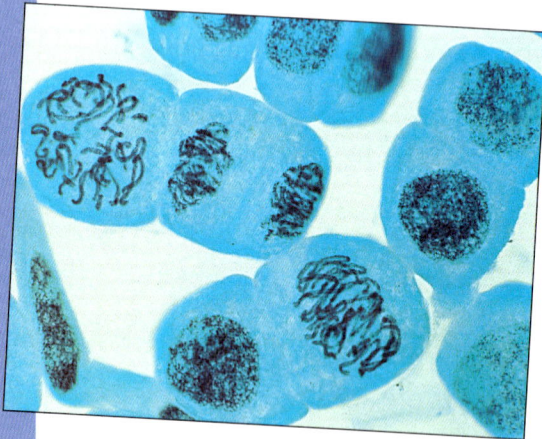

Genes

The features of both plants and animals are controlled by their **genes**. Genes are found on thread-like structures called **chromosomes**, which are in the nucleus of every living cell.

You can only see the chromosomes when a cell is dividing, like these onion cells.

Different genes control different features. For example, in wheat, different genes control important crop features such as the number and size of the grains, the nutrients in the grain, the length of the stalk and the ability to withstand drought.

This photograph shows wheat plants with different genes for the length of the stalk.

1 What else apart from genes do you think might affect a plant's stalk length?

2 How could a plant breeder be sure that differences in stalk length were caused by different genes?

Bred for bread

Flour is produced from wheat grains with particular features. Different wheats produce flours with particular textures or flavours. To make certain types of flour, wheat grains are carefully blended before grinding. New strains of wheat are continually being bred to produce improved flours and bread.

Choosing the right genes

Breeding wheat with particular characteristics involves selecting the genes for certain features and combining them in a plant that will grow well. This takes a great deal of time and care.

The first step in a breeding programme is to look at different wheat plants. The plants will not be identical – they will show variation, because of their different genes.

The next step is to find a collection of plants which have between them features close to those required. The cells of these plants will contain chromosomes that carry genes for those features.

These selected plants are then bred together. The grains produced are planted and the process repeated for several generations until enough grains with the required features are produced, on a suitably strong plant.

Breeding programmes can also be used to 'breed out' undesirable features, such as weak stems, low resistance to disease or poor growth rate.

Choose wheat plants which:
• produce large numbers of grains
• produce large grains
• have a strong stem

Breed together in various combinations and grow plants from the resulting seeds

Collect the grain from plants with the desired features and grow them for several generations, continuing to cross-breed as necessary

Mutations

Changes in genes also take place naturally, by chance. These changes are called **mutations**. Some mutations can be harmful, but others are useful. Plant breeders are always on the lookout for useful mutations so that they can breed better plants – better 'green machines'.

Imagine that you are a plant breeder. You have been asked to breed an onion which, when peeled, does not make you cry. Write a plan showing how you would go about this, and saying what other features you would try to include in your new onion.

CHAINED TOGETHER

'Did you get all this food from your allotment?' Ralph asked. 'All the vegetables, but not the chicken,' said Carl. 'But I expect we could keep chickens too if we tried. Why don't we have a go, Dad?'
'The foxes would get them,' said his dad.

Feeding patterns

Foxes are **carnivores**. They eat meat. Their digestive systems are specialized to deal with the flesh of other animals. They would not survive on a diet of plants alone.

Chickens are **herbivores**. They eat plant material.

Human beings are **omnivores**. Our digestive systems can cope equally well with animal or plant material.

Producers and consumers

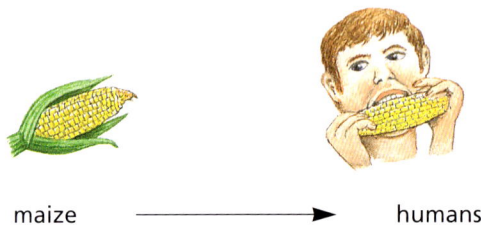

We can show these relationships in diagrams called **food chains**.

All animals are **consumers**. They cannot make food for themselves. They have to eat other organisms – either plants or animals.

maize   ⟶   humans

maize   ⟶   chickens   ⟶   humans

maize   ⟶   chickens   ⟶   foxes

At the start of each food chain is a plant. Plants are at the base of all food chains, because they produce their own food by the process of photosynthesis. Plants are known as **producers**. They produce the food that other organisms consume.

Copy these two food chains and suggest organisms that could fill the gaps.

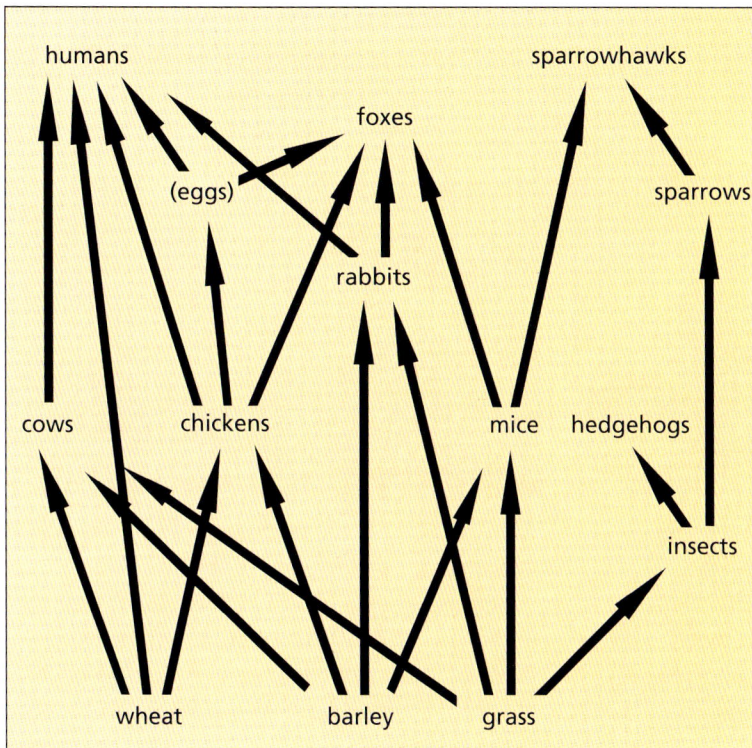

? ⟶ caterpillar ⟶ thrush ⟶ sparrowhawk

microscopic algae ⟶ water fleas ⟶ **?** ⟶ perch ⟶ pike

The web of life

Very few animals depend on only one type of organism for their food. Carnivorous animals may eat two or three different animals. Also, each type of organism may be eaten by several different animals.

◀ *We can show the way the feeding patterns interconnect in a diagram called a* **food web**.

Use the food web to construct three different food chains. Label each organism in the chain as either a producer or a consumer.

Look at the meal in the photograph. Make a list showing which foods come from consumers and which from producers.

humans   sparrowhawks
foxes
(eggs)   sparrows
rabbits
cows   chickens   mice   hedgehogs
insects
wheat   barley   grass

9

SLUGGED OUT

'This cabbage has been really badly eaten,' said Carl.
'The slugs have got it,' said his dad.
'I've never known a year so bad.'

'Why are there so many slugs this year?' asked Carl.
'It could be because it's so wet. The conditions have been ideal for slugs to move around and to breed.'

Carl spoke to Mr Ashton at the Society Hut, who said 'It was very wet in '84 and '87, but I don't remember there being so many slugs then.'

Miss Maguire had a slug problem on her allotment too.
'The slugs seem right out of control this year. There's nothing eating them.'
'What normally eats them?' asked Carl.

'During the day it's birds, and at night hedgehogs,' replied Miss Maguire.
'That explains it then,' said Carl. 'We've been too good at scaring birds away. And remember that family of dead hedgehogs we saw? There are always squashed hedgehogs on the road, too.'

'Surely a few birds and hedgehogs wouldn't make such a difference to the cabbages?'
'Yes they would,' said Carl's dad. 'You would be surprised how many slugs a hedgehog can eat in a night. There's not much energy in a slug so they have to eat lots of them.'

GREEN MACHINE

10

Chomping through the cabbages

1 What was Carl's dad's first idea about the cause of the increase in slugs?

2 What evidence suggested that his idea was wrong?

Draw a food web showing the feeding links between cabbages, slugs, birds and hedgehogs.

Use your diagram to explain why more cabbages are eaten if the number of hedgehogs is reduced.

How many hedgehogs?

Plants make their own food by photosynthesis and are producers. Slugs eat cabbage plants. Slugs are **primary consumers** – they are the first animal in the food chain to eat the plants.

Slugs eat plants, such as cabbages, to provide them with the energy they need to stay alive and move around. Inside a slug's body, the cabbage takes part in chemical reactions to make new materials. Some of these materials become part of the slug's body, and the slug **excretes** (gets rid of) the rest as waste. The materials in the slug's body take part in more chemical reactions to release energy. The waste materials from these reactions are excreted. Overall, if the slug is not growing, the material that it eats is balanced by the material that it excretes. A growing slug eats more material than it excretes. Not all the energy in the cabbage is transferred to the slug, some of it remains in the waste material. So slugs have to eat a lot of cabbage just to stay alive, and growing slugs need to eat even more.

Hedgehogs prey on slugs. They are **secondary consumers** – they eat primary consumers. Just as slugs eat cabbage, hedgehogs eat slugs to give them energy. They need the energy mainly for keeping warm and moving around. When a hedgehog eats a slug, some of the energy from the slug's body is transferred to the hedgehog and some is excreted in waste material. A hedgehog might need a daily diet of 100 slugs just to get enough energy to stay alive and a growing hedgehog needs to eat even more.

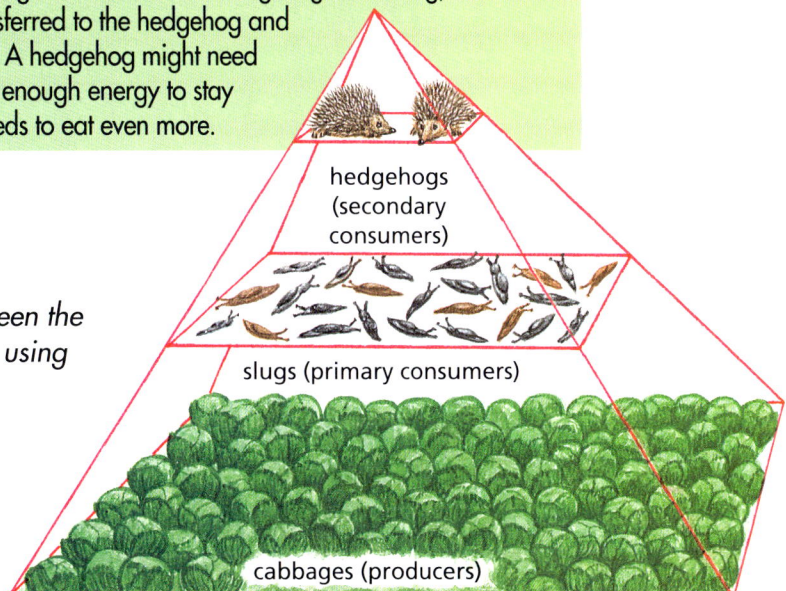

Pyramids of numbers

*We can show the feeding relationships between the numbers of cabbages, slugs and hedgehogs using a diagram called a **pyramid of numbers**.*

Use the pyramid of numbers to explain why a small reduction in the number of hedgehogs can result in a large increase in slug damage to cabbages.

hedgehogs (secondary consumers)

slugs (primary consumers)

cabbages (producers)

BUILDING

Then …

The great pyramids of Egypt were built about 4500 years ago.

Hagia Sophia in Istanbul was built between AD 532 and 537.

York Minster was begun in 1291 and took over 200 years to finish.

All these buildings were made before the days of powered machinery. They all involved moving and lifting vast quantities of materials.

Make a rough estimate of the height of each of these buildings.

How do you think people managed to move and lift the materials for these buildings? Discuss your ideas.

... and now

These pictures show two different building sites.
Building tasks may involve:
- lifting
- digging
- moving building materials and earth
- supporting part of a building
- supporting people and machinery on soft ground.

How might each of these tasks be made easier on the building sites? Discuss your ideas, and make a note of them.

1 Which of the techniques you have listed need powered machinery? Which may have been used for the buildings on the opposite page?

2 What differences do you think powered machinery may have made to:

● the time taken to complete a building

● the number of people involved in building?

In this unit, you will learn about the science behind many of the techniques shown on this page.

A ROOF OVER YOUR HEAD

Pitched or flat?

These pictures show some of the types of roof used for houses built at different times and in different places.

List the advantages and disadvantages of:

● a pitched (sloping) roof

● a flat roof.

1 Which sort of roof do you think would be best for a house in:

● a hot, dry place

● somewhere with a lot of rain?

Do a survey of house roof types in your neighbourhood. You could count the houses with flat roofs and with pitched roofs, or you might decide to divide up the pitched roofs into different types.

Make a poster to display your results.

Look at the roofs of other buildings in your neighbourhood – such as schools, garages, barns, shops, blocks of flats and factories.

Suggest reasons for different buildings having different types of roof.

How roofs are constructed

Many modern houses have roofs made from ready-assembled sections. These pictures show four different designs of these sections.

An older house would probably have a roof made of two large strong wooden beams called **purlins**, set into the bricks at either end. Smaller beams called **rafters** are laid on the purlins.

A typical older house roof might have 13 pairs of rafters laid along two purlins.

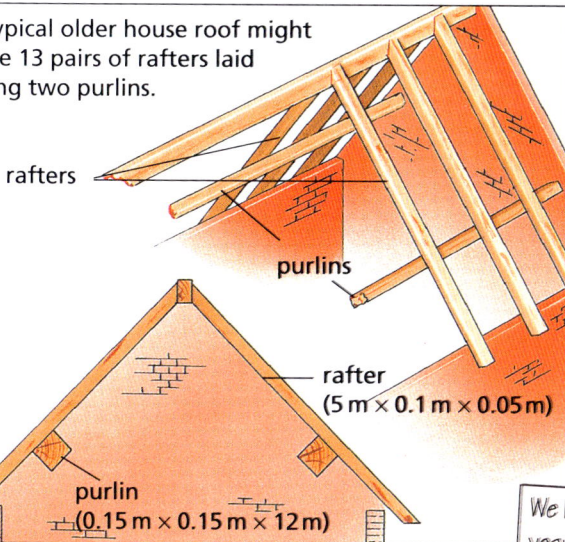

rafters

purlins

rafter
(5 m × 0.1 m × 0.05 m)

purlin
(0.15 m × 0.15 m × 12 m)

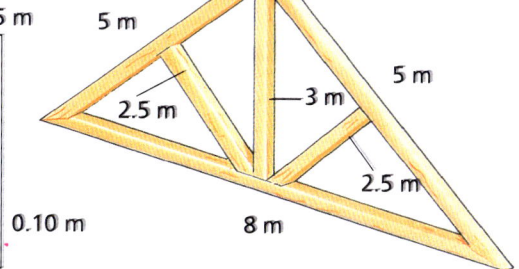

0.025 m   5 m

2.5 m   3 m   5 m

                       2.5 m

0.10 m   8 m

A newer house roof might have 13 ready-made sections. The timber used to make the sections usually has a cross-section 0.10 m by 0.025 m. It is referred to as '4 by 1' because of its size in inches – 4 inches by 1 inch.

Ask an expert

Gary's dad is a builder. He was asked to be the 'expert' on a local radio phone-in on house improvements. Here are one caller's story and questions. ▶

2   What do you think Gary's dad said in reply to these questions? Use the information on this page to help you write an answer.

We have some friends who live in a house like ours, but it's a few years older. Our friends have just put an extension into the attic of their house. We had been thinking about doing something like this, so we got a builder to give us an estimate of the cost. When the builder looked in our roof, she said: 'There's no way you can put an extension into your attic. It's not like older houses where there was plenty of space. There's so much wood in these attics it's like Sherwood Forest when you get up there!' I asked the builder why they put more wood in modern roofs when wood is so expensive. She said there was actually less wood in a modern roof than in an older roof.
I'd like to know two things. How is my roof different from our friends' roof? And how come there's less wood up there when there looks to be so much more?

LEVERS

The pictures on these two pages show different sorts of levers. Some are simple, others more complicated. They all make jobs easier to do.

How levers work

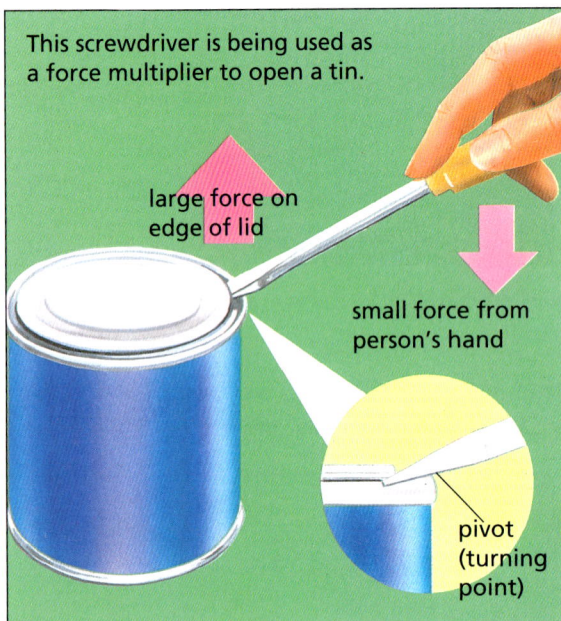

Levers work in one of two ways.
- They convert a small force into a bigger force – they are **force multipliers**, or
- They convert a small movement into a bigger movement – they are **distance multipliers**.

This screwdriver is being used as a force multiplier to open a tin.

large force on edge of lid

small force from person's hand

pivot (turning point)

This fishing rod is being used as a distance multiplier to lift fish out of the water.

large movement

small movement

pivot

The pictures on the opposite page show many different levers in use.

◼ List as many levers as you can find in the pictures. For each one, decide whether it is a force multiplier or a distance multiplier.

◼ Draw sketches of at least three of the levers shown opposite. In each one, mark the **pivot** (the point around which the lever turns).

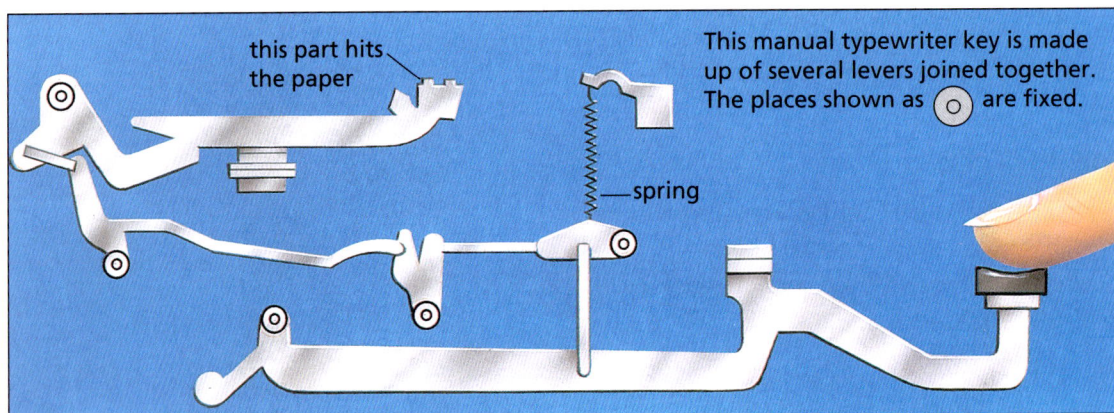

this part hits the paper

spring

This manual typewriter key is made up of several levers joined together. The places shown as ⊙ are fixed.

◼ Study the picture above carefully and try to work out what happens when someone presses the key.

16

WATER IN ... WATER OUT

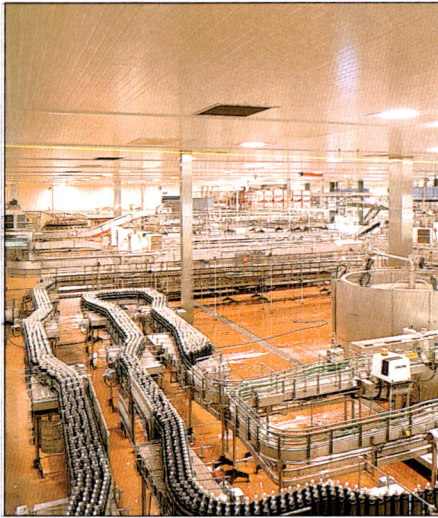

Coca-Cola

This Coca-Cola factory makes over 600 million litres of soft drinks per year.
A can of Coca-Cola contains one-third of a litre.

1 How many cans would the factory's yearly output fill?

The factory takes in 400 000 litres of water per hour. Some of this water is used for the **product** – it ends up in the drink. Some of it is used for the **process** of making the drink.

2 The process water does not end up in the drink. What do you think it is used for?

A question of balance

Average daily intake (cm³)		Average daily output (cm³)	
Drink	1300	Urine	1500
Food	850	Breath	400
Formed during respiration	350	Sweat	500
		Faeces	100
Total	2500	Total	2500

(2500 cm³ is 2½ litres = approximately 4½ pints.)

Each day you lose about 2 litres of water through sweating and urinating. So each day you have to replace this water.

- Make a list of the drinks you have in a typical day, and when you drink them.

  Compare your list with others in your group.

3 How much of your drink intake is water and how much is other drinks made from water?

Your daily intake will probably total less than 2 litres, because you take in a lot of water in food. A typical daily balance sheet for water is shown in the table.

4 What do you think would happen if your daily intake and output of water did not balance?

The water in your body

About 60 – 70% of your body mass is made up of water.

One litre of water has a mass of 1 kg.

- Work out approximately the mass of water contained in your body.

- Work out approximately what volume of water your body contains.

5 How many Coca-Cola cans would it fill?

The importance of water

Many chemical changes take place in your body during processes such as digestion and respiration. For these changes to occur the substances must be dissolved in water.

People can live for 50 – 60 days without food, but will die after a few days without water.

Milk

Coca-Cola is made by adding various ingredients to water. Milk contains a large proportion of water.

Milk is about 90% water by mass. A milk cow will drink about 45 litres of water a day. Cows are milked twice a day, once early in the morning and again in the evening. About 36 litres of milk can be obtained from a milk cow each day (about 64 pints).

6 What proportion of a cow's drinking water ends up in milk? What other sources of water does a cow have?

If cows do not have enough water to drink, they do not produce any milk.

Supplying water

We are fortunate in Britain because we have a good supply of water piped to our homes. Occasionally we have a hosepipe ban, but this is a minor problem compared with the water shortages in some parts of the world.

- Look at the rainfall patterns in Bombay, London and Swakopmund (in south-west Africa).

- Plot bar graphs and suggest how the water supply problems are different in Bombay, London and Swakopmund.

Rainfall (mm) in Bombay, London and Swakopmund (SW Africa)

	Bombay	London	Swakopmund
Jan	3	55	0
Feb	0	45	3
Mar	3	40	5
Apr	0	50	0
May	20	50	0
Jun	520	40	0
Jul	700	50	0
Aug	400	50	0
Sep	300	40	0
Oct	60	55	3
Nov	10	60	0
Dec	0	50	5

THE WATER CYCLE

Where does it come from?

In Britain, most people live quite close to a river. Water which has fallen as rain over a large area of the country finds its way into rivers. In most rivers, the water flows all year round.

Water vapour condenses to form clouds.

Where does it go?

All rivers flow eventually to the sea. In spite of all this water flowing into the sea, the level of water in the sea remains fairly constant. This is because water is continually escaping from the surface of the sea as water vapour. This water vapour then forms clouds which produce more rain over the land. The rainwater finds it way into rivers and then returns to the sea. The water goes round and round this water cycle.

2 What does 'condense' mean? Why does the water vapour condense to form clouds?

By the time you have finished this unit you should be able to explain the water cycle in detail. But first, study this diagram of the water cycle and discuss your ideas about it. Use the questions in the boxes as a framework for your discussion. Start at the sea.

Water evaporates from the sea.

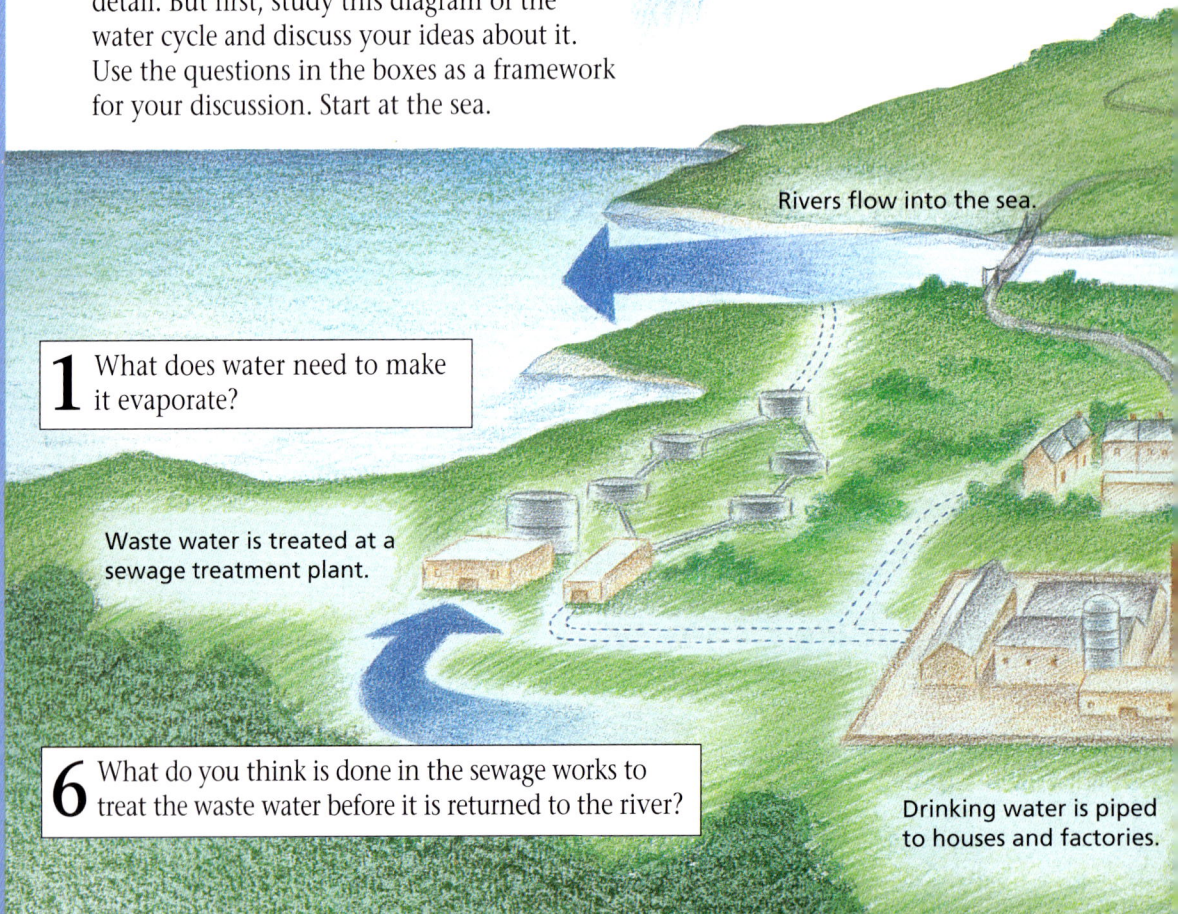

Rivers flow into the sea.

1 What does water need to make it evaporate?

Waste water is treated at a sewage treatment plant.

6 What do you think is done in the sewage works to treat the waste water before it is returned to the river?

Drinking water is piped to houses and factories.

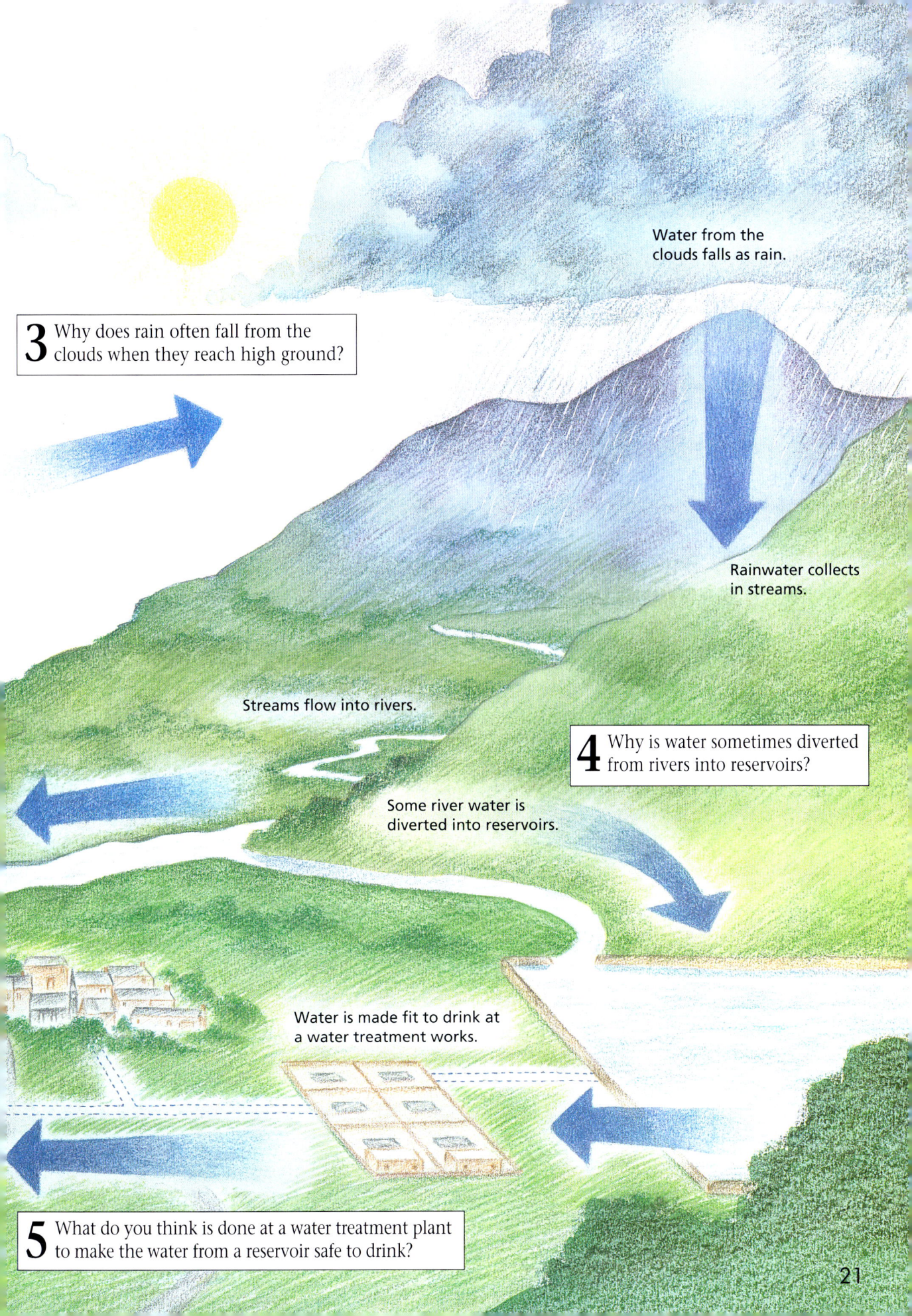

Water from the
clouds falls as rain.

3 Why does rain often fall from the
clouds when they reach high ground?

Rainwater collects
in streams.

Streams flow into rivers.

4 Why is water sometimes diverted
from rivers into reservoirs?

Some river water is
diverted into reservoirs.

Water is made fit to drink at
a water treatment works.

5 What do you think is done at a water treatment plant
to make the water from a reservoir safe to drink?

A THREE-PART STORY

Part 1 – tiny particles

Gary and the others went to Miss Grant's lesson about how drinks spread out when you mix them with water.

> We can see that coloured drinks spread out.

> We can smell Miss Grant's perfume when she walks into the room. Bits of the perfume must spread out throughout the room.

> We need a theory or idea which explains this evidence.

Part 2 – spacing and movement

The next lesson was to be about solids, liquids and gases.

> This bag is definitely solid!

> This drink is a liquid ...

> ... and there's gas in this football.

Part 3 – now you see it ...

Gary and the others were thinking about how solids can change into liquids and back again, and liquids can change into gases and back again.

> When you heat a solid to a high enough temperature it melts.

> When you heat a liquid to a high enough temperature it boils.

Discuss how you would answer the questions raised at the end of each lesson.

There must be lots of bits of perfume escaping from Miss Grant because we can smell it all over the room.

I expect she only puts on a few drops, so each bit must be very, very small.

The first part of the theory is that everything consists of very tiny particles.

Can we use this idea of particles to explain what happens when tea is made?

... and Bovril?

... and when blackcurrant drink is diluted?

We know that solids, liquids and gases have different densities and different shapes or squashabilities.

If they all consist of particles, maybe the theory can explain the differences...

The second part of the theory is that:
- in a solid the particles are close together in fixed positions.
- in a liquid the particles are close together, but they can move around inside the liquid.
- in a gas the particles are much more widely spaced and can move around anywhere inside the container.

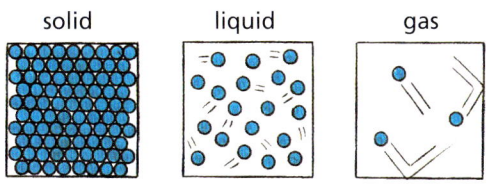

I wonder how this part of the theory explains the different properties of solids ...

... and liquids?

... and gases?

solid   liquid   gas

The third part of the theory is that when a substance is heated, energy is transferred to the particles. This energy causes the particles to move more vigorously.
- In a solid the particles begin to vibrate more vigorously until the regular pattern of the solid is broken down and the particles become free to move around.
- In a liquid the particles eventually gain sufficient energy to escape from the liquid.

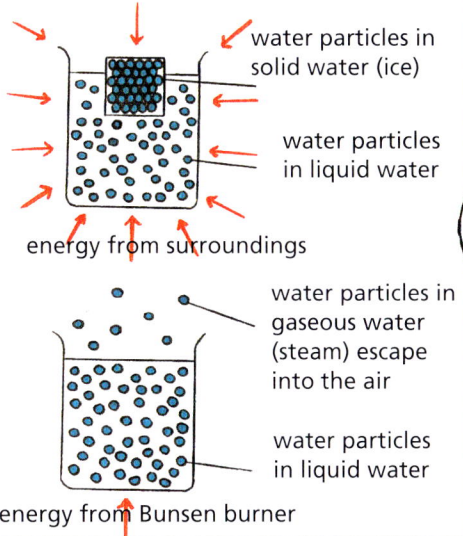

water particles in solid water (ice)

water particles in liquid water

energy from surroundings

water particles in gaseous water (steam) escape into the air

water particles in liquid water

energy from Bunsen burner

I wonder how this part of the theory explains what happens when a gas is cooled?

... and when a liquid is cooled?

BREWING

The pictures on this page show different stages in the production of beer.

> Use this information and any other you can find to make a poster or a display about brewing.

● You could start by making lists of the raw materials and products for a brewery.

● You might be able to find pictures to cut out of magazines. A flow chart of the process might help.

Beer production

1 Malting

Moist barley is allowed to germinate. This starts to convert the starch in the barley into sugars.

After a couple of days the germination is stopped by heating the barley in a kiln. The product, which is called **malt,** is then ground up to a flour called **grist**.

2 Mashing

The grist is taken to the brewery. It is mixed with water and warmed. This completes the conversion of starch to sugars.

The sugar solution is called **wort**. What is left of the grain is filtered off. This lorry is taking it away for use as animal feed.

3 Boiling

Hops, which are grown in the South East of England, give the beer its bitter flavour.

The wort is mixed with hops and boiled in large tanks.

4 Fermentation

The liquid is separated from what is left of the hops, cooled and transferred to a large fermenter. Yeast is added and this speeds up the fermentation. The sugars are converted to alcohol and carbon dioxide.

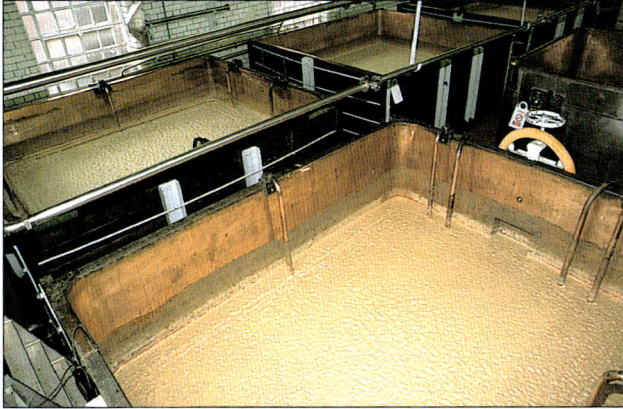

Fermenters used to be open tanks, but now very large conical vessels are used.
◀ The froth on the surface of this old-fashioned open tank is caused by carbon dioxide bubbling off. In a modern fermenter the carbon dioxide is pumped away as it forms and used later to add fizz to some beers.

5 Conditioning

Each type of beer is then stored for a particular length of time under carefully controlled conditions. This lorry is delivering casks, kegs, bottles and tins of beer to a pub.

enzymes in barley			
starch ⟶ sugars			
Malting		Mashing	Boiling
Germinating	Kilning		
15 – 20 °C	60 – 100 °C	64 °C	100 °C
2 days	2 days	1 – 2 hours	1 – 2 hours

enzymes in added yeast	
sugars ⟶ alcohol + carbon dioxide + heat	
Fermenting	
10 – 12 °C (lager)	18 – 20 °C (ale)
7 or more days	

Conditioning
1 – 4 weeks

Brewing in a nutshell

□ Look at the diagram below. Sketch a temperature against time graph for the brewing process.

□ Mark on the graph the stages where enzymes are used to catalyse reactions.

Different enzymes work better at different temperatures.

1 Why do you think the fermenter needs to be cooled?

SEEING STARS

A group of stars called the Pleiades, photographed through a powerful telescope.

Star gazing

For thousands of years, people have studied the stars. Stars have been used to keep track of time, and to guide sailors at sea. Modern spacecraft are guided by stars as they travel between the planets. Astronomers nowadays use powerful telescopes to help them find out more about the stars.

Astronomers are scientists who study objects in space. They do experiments on earth to help explain what they see through their telescopes.

Star groups

This map shows some of the brightest stars in the northern part of the sky.

Some stars appear to be grouped together. A group of stars is called a **constellation**. The constellations shown in the map here can be seen at all times of night, all through the year. In the southern part of the sky, different constellations come into view at different times.

Great Bear

Little Bear

Cassiopeia

Polaris

- If you can find a safe place with a good view of the night sky, try to find some of the constellations. Start by looking for the Great Bear (also called the Plough or the Dipper), the Little Bear and Cassiopeia.

- Keep a record of the constellations that you can see.

Swan

Eagle

Scorpion

Orion the Hunter

Large Dog

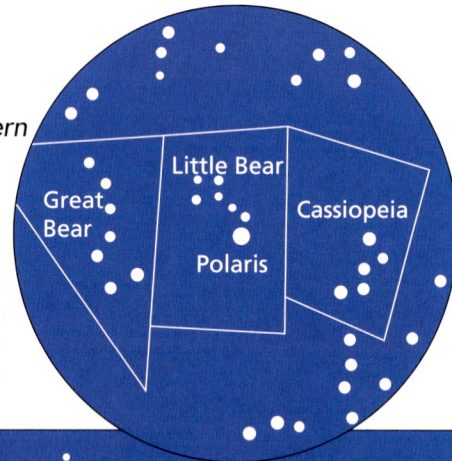

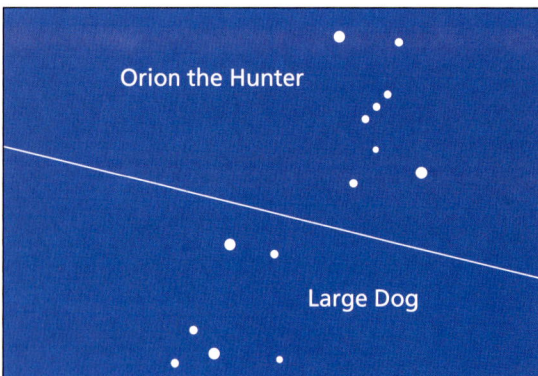

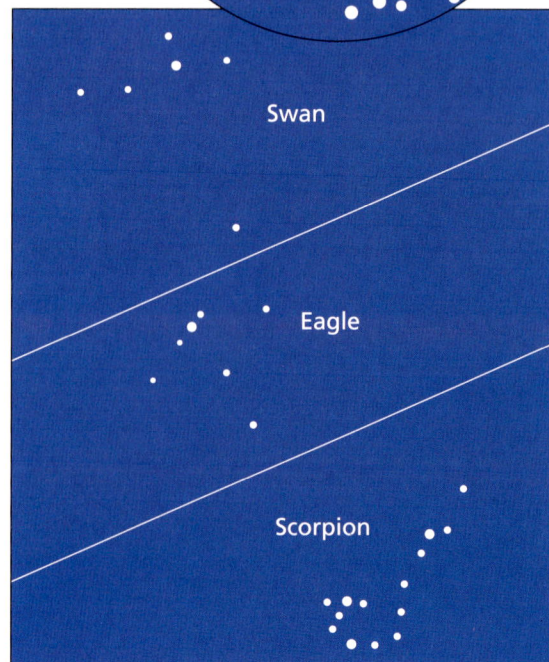

These constellations can be be seen from Britain only at certain times.

Lives of the stars

With some imagination, constellations can be made to represent people and animals. The Ancient Greeks named constellations after characters from their traditional stories.

- Try to find Orion or the Scorpion (Scorpius) in the night sky. You can see Orion in winter, and Scorpius in summer – you will not see both at once.

- Read the story of the Hunter and the Scorpion. Use library books to find more Greek stories about the stars. You could start with Hercules or Andromeda.

The Hunter and the Scorpion

Orion was part god, part human. He was a great hunter, and often boasted of his skills. One day Diana, the goddess of hunting, challenged him to a hunting contest. Orion killed many animals but, as he was showing them off to Diana, a scorpion stung him. As he lay dying from the sting Zeus, king of the gods, took pity on him. He placed Orion in the sky as a group of stars with his dogs for company. He made the scorpion into another group of stars – and put him as far away from Orion as possible.

Another way of looking at it

Constellations are a useful way of describing parts of the sky, but they are not 'real'. Different people see different 'pictures' in the stars. This 800-year-old Chinese star map shows some constellations used in the Far East at that time. Most of them are different from those used by the ancient Greeks and by us today.

Astrology – science or superstition?

Some people think that stars affect our lives. **Astrologers** write **horoscopes** that predict what will happen to people. They use 'star signs' to make their predictions.

- Plan and carry out an investigation to find out whether astrologers' predictions come true. You could use horoscopes from newspapers or magazines.

Scientists use **theories** to make **predictions** that they test in **experiments**. If the predictions do not come true, they know that the theories must be wrong so they try to develop better ones.

- Discuss whether you think astrologers are scientists.

- Use the results of your investigation to plan a magazine article called 'Astrology – science or superstition?'.

Aquarius 21 Jan – 18 Feb	Pisces 19 Feb – 20 Mar	Aries 21 Mar – 20 Apr
Taurus 21 Apr – 21 May	Gemini 22 May – 21 Jun	Cancer 22 Jun – 22 Jul
Leo 23 Jul – 23 Aug	Virgo 24 Aug – 22 Sep	Libra 23 Sep – 22 Oct
Scorpio 23 Oct – 22 Nov	Sagittarius 23 Nov – 21 Dec	Capricorn 22 Dec – 20 Jan

STARS AND STRIPES

Star streaks

If you look at the stars at different times during the night, they appear to move slowly across the sky.

The pictures on this page are long-exposure photographs of the night sky. To take them, a camera was fixed pointing at one part of the sky with its shutter held open for about an hour or more. Each star makes a long thin streak on the photograph.

■ Look at the ends of the star streaks and find the stars that made up the constellations. (Look at pages 26–7 to remind yourself of their shapes.)

1 How can you tell from the photographs that the camera was kept pointing at the same part of the sky?

Orion

Cassiopeia

Going round in circles

Photographing the stars from earth is rather like taking a photograph from a spinning roundabout. The stars actually stay still, but they make streaks on the photograph because the earth is spinning.

Polaris is a bright star in the Little Bear. It is almost directly above the north pole of the earth, so it does not appear to move. The other stars appear to move in circles with Polaris at the centre.

Polaris

Little Bear

Great Bear

The earth takes 24 hours to make one complete turn about its axis. Draw the star streaks that you would expect to see on a 6-hour photograph of the Great Bear and Little Bear.

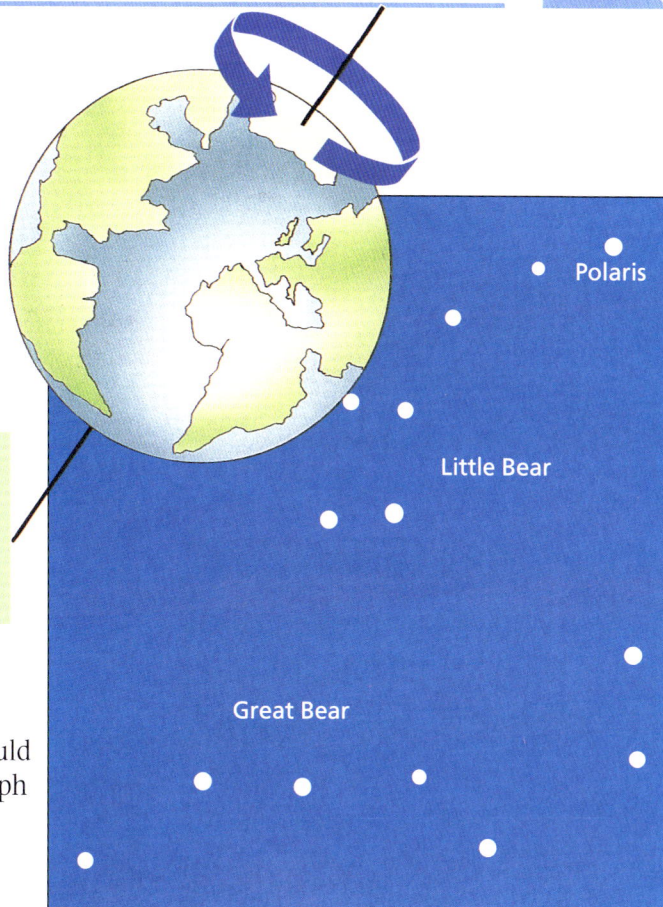

The light from this bulb comes from its hot wire filament. It is connected to a variable power supply.

Red, white and blue

Stars are very hot balls of gas. The light that any hot object gives out depends on its temperature.

Raising the temperature of a hot object makes its light brighter, and changes its colour from red to blue-white.

The coolest stars are red-white, with temperatures of about 3000 °C, and the hottest are blue-white, with temperatures of over 10 000 °C. Stars like our sun are yellow-white and have temperatures of about 6000 °C.

There is one red-white star, called Betelgeuse, in Orion. The other stars in Orion are blue-white. Try to find Betelgeuse in the star streak opposite.

2 As well as temperature, what else do you think affects a star's brightness as viewed by us on earth? Discuss your ideas.

29

MORE THAN MEETS THE EYE

Visible light is only a small part of the radiation given out by stars and other objects in space. It is part of a family of radiation called **electromagnetic radiation**. All members of the family have waves that travel through space at 300 million metres per second (nearly 700 million miles per hour).

Gamma rays	X-rays	Ultraviolet

Gamma rays

Satellite studies

Astronomers use special telescopes in orbit high above the earth's atmosphere to study gamma rays, X-rays and ultraviolet from objects in space.

Ultraviolet

High-factor protection

The sun's ultraviolet radiation can give us sunburn, but the earth's atmosphere protects us from most of the other harmful radiation given out by the sun.

Visible light

Exploding stars

Astronomers study many objects apart from stars. About 900 years ago a star in the constellation of Taurus exploded. Chinese astronomers saw it as a very bright 'new star' (called a **supernova**) that faded away over a few months.

This cloud of hot gas is the remains of the explosion. It is called the Crab Nebula ('**nebula**' means 'cloud').

Look up 'supernova' in an encyclopedia and find out when people have seen these exploding stars.

- For each type of electromagnetic radiation shown on these two pages, list at least one situation where it is used on earth.

- Use library books and encyclopedias to find out more about one type of electromagnetic radiation and its uses.

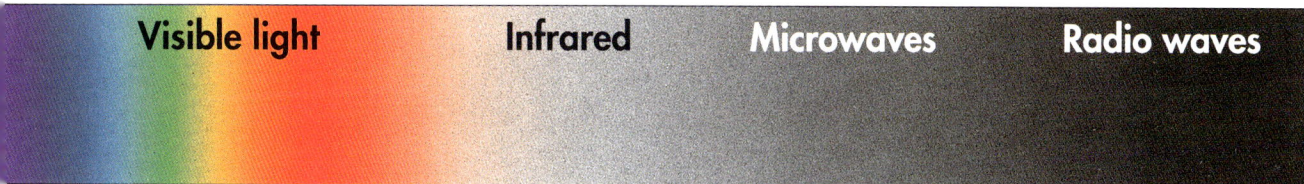

| Visible light | Infrared | Microwaves | Radio waves |

Not to scale

Visible light | **The Orion Nebula**

Infrared | **Warming up**

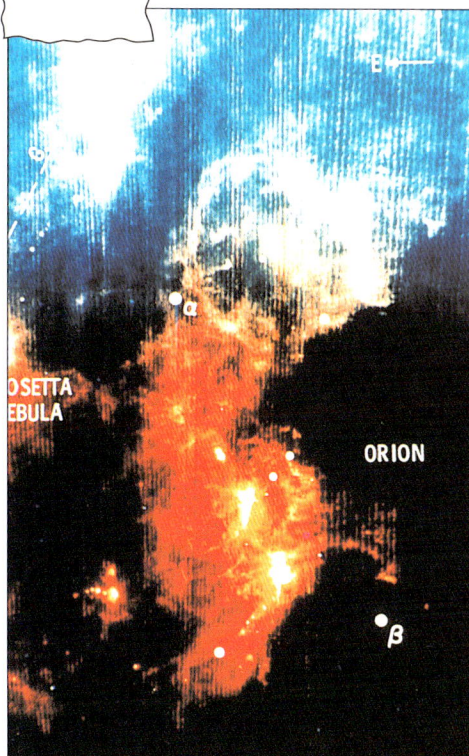

Infrared radiation comes from warm objects. You can feel it coming from an electric heater as it heats up, before you see the red glow.
Infrared radiation from the sun keeps the earth warm.
An infrared-sensitive telescope shows that there are clouds of warm gas between the stars. The gas in Orion appears to be clumping together gradually and warming up to make new stars.

If you look through binoculars at the 'stars' in Orion's sword you can see that one is in fact a gas cloud – it looks bigger and fuzzier than a star. It is called the Orion Nebula.

- If you can find a safe place that gives a good view of Orion, look for the nebula in his sword.

Radio waves | **Radio pictures**

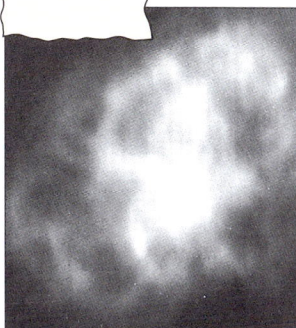

This picture was made by a computer. It shows radio waves from the Crab Nebula.

- Compare this picture with the photograph showing visible light from the Crab Nebula. In what ways are they similar? In what ways are they different? Discuss your ideas.

31

IS THERE ANYONE OUT THERE?

Science fiction …

In the film *ET*, an extraterrestrial creature visited earth. ('Extraterrestrial' means 'outside earth'.)

Is the earth the only planet where there is life? Many people have imagined what creatures from other planets might be like …

Sometimes creatures from other planets are imagined to look very like human beings.

A big greyish rounded bulk, the size, perhaps, of a bear, was rising slowly and painfully out of the cylinder. As it bulged up and caught the light, it glistened like wet leather.

Two large dark-coloured eyes were regarding me steadfastly. The mass that framed them, the head of the thing, it was rounded, and had, one might say, a face. There was a mouth under the eyes, the lipless brim of which quivered and panted, and dropped saliva. The whole creature heaved and pulsated convulsively. A lank tentacular appendary gripped the edge of the cylinder, another swayed in the air.

Those who have never seen a living Martian can scarcely imagine the strange horror of its appearance. The peculiar V-shaped mouth with its pointed upper lip, the absence of brow ridges, the absence of a chin beneath the wedge-like lower lip, the incessant quivering of this mouth, the Gorgon group of tentacles, the tumultuous breathing of the lungs in a strange atmosphere, the evident heaviness and painfulness of movement due to the greater gravitational energy of the earth – above all, the extraordinary intensity of the immense eyes – were at once vital, intense, inhuman, crippled and monstrous. There was something fungoid in the oily brown skin, something in the clumsy deliberation of the tedious movements unspeakably nasty. Even at this first encounter, this first glimpse, I was overcome with disgust and dread.

In The War of the Worlds, *written in 1898, H G Wells imagined a creature from Mars landing on earth. You'll probably need a dictionary to look up the unusual words he used to describe this imaginary creature.*

- List any other examples of imaginary extraterrestrial life-forms that you know of from books or films.

Is it alive?

All life-forms, real or imaginary, have some important things in common.

- Choose one imaginary creature (from this page, or from somewhere else) and list all the 'clues' that tell you it is alive.

- Invent your own 'creature from another planet'. Write a short story about your creature and use it to make a poster. Make sure your poster and story contain several 'clues' that show the creature is alive.

... and fact

Astronomers study the planets using telescopes. Unmanned space probes have landed on Mars and Venus, and flown close to Mercury, Jupiter, Saturn, Uranus and Neptune. None has found any signs of life.

Venus

The *Voyager 2* space probe was launched by the USA in 1977. In 1979 it flew past **Jupiter**, and then on to **Saturn** (1981), **Uranus** (1986) and **Neptune** (1989). All these planets are very cold (their surfaces never reach 0 °C) and are made mainly of hydrogen gas. There may be liquid or solid material deep in their centres.

Mercury is the closest planet to the sun. It has no atmosphere. The side facing the sun can reach temperatures of 400 °C, but the temperature on the dark side drops to −170 °C.

Venus has a thick choking atmosphere of carbon dioxide, with clouds of sulphuric acid droplets. It is very hot all over, about 500 °C.

Mars has a very thin atmosphere of carbon dioxide. It is very cold – the temperature never gets above about 7 °C, and is generally about −90 °C.

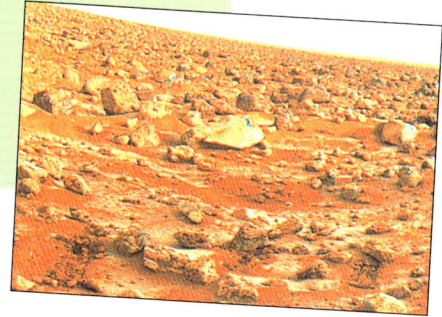

The two Russian Venera *spacecraft that landed on Venus in 1982 survived for about an hour before being destroyed by the harsh conditions there. American* Mariner *and* Viking *spacecraft studied Mars in the 1960s.*

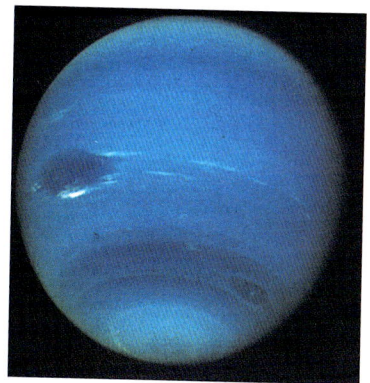

A *Voyager 2* picture of Jupiter ...   ... and Neptune.

A good home?

For each planet mentioned on this page, list what might make it difficult for any creature to live there.

The American space agency NASA is discussing plans to send people to Mars.

What problems do you think there would be for people visiting Mars, or any other planets? Discuss the problems involved in:

● travelling to other planets

● surviving on other planets.

No spacecraft has yet flown close to Pluto. It is too far away to study in detail through a telescope, but astronomers are fairly sure that it is a small, solid planet.

What do you think it would be like to land on Pluto? Write a short account of your ideas and draw a picture showing what you think Pluto may be like.

FAR OUT

The Milky Way – our galaxy

Astronomers have mapped the positions of stars and gas clouds in our galaxy to make this picture. It shows what the Milky Way galaxy would look like if we could see it from the outside.

We see the Milky Way as a faint band of light across the sky. It is made up of millions of stars, too faint to see individually without a telescope. These stars, and our sun, are part of a huge group of stars called a **galaxy**. This galaxy is sometimes called the Milky Way galaxy. It contains over a hundred thousand million stars. There are billions of other galaxies.

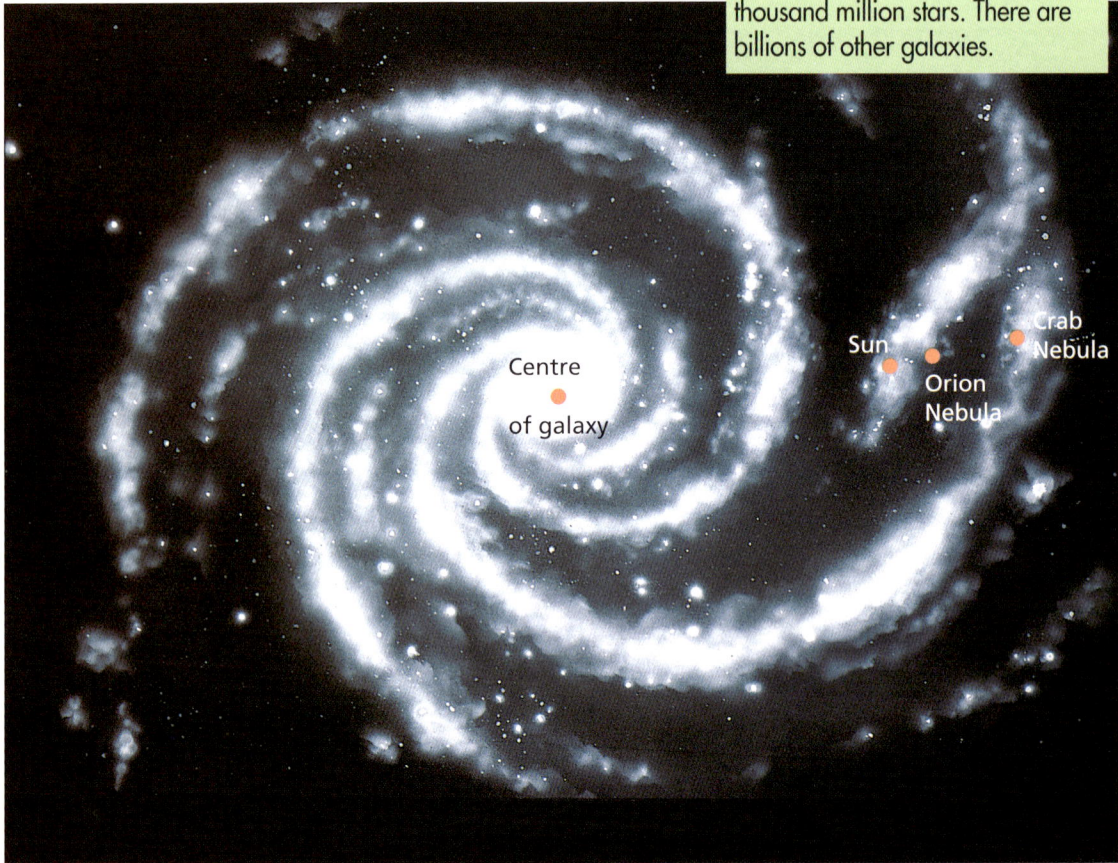

Centre of galaxy

Sun

Orion Nebula

Crab Nebula

Astronomical distances

A **light year** is the distance that light travels in one year – about 10 million million kilometres.

Apart from the sun, the nearest star to the earth is 4¼ light years away. Most of the bright stars in our sky are hundreds of light years away from us. The solar system is about 30 000 light years from the centre of the Milky Way galaxy.

Roughly how far is it (in light years):

● from the solar system to the Orion Nebula

● from one side of the Milky Way to the other?

Other galaxies in the universe

Galaxies are grouped into **clusters**. The Milky Way is one of a group of galaxies centred on the Virgo Cluster which contains thousands of galaxies. There are many other clusters in the **universe**.
The universe is all the matter, space and energy that exist – it is everything there is, anywhere.

◀ The Magellanic Clouds are two small galaxies close to our own. They can be seen from south of the equator as small fuzzy clouds in the night sky. The Portuguese explorer Magellan discovered them on his voyage round the world in 1521. This is the Large Magellanic Cloud.

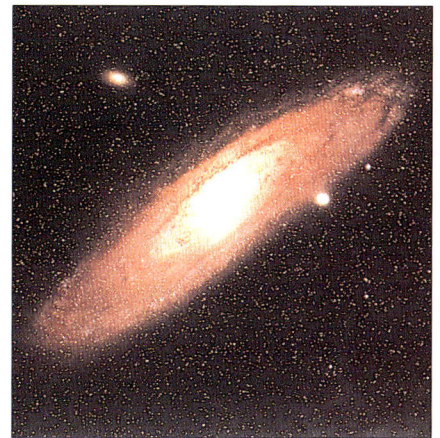

This picture shows what our galaxy and its surroundings would look like from a distance of many million light years.

This galaxy is about 2¼ million light years away. It appears as a small faint patch of light in the constellation of Andromeda, and is sometimes called the Andromeda Nebula. It is the most distant object that can be seen from earth with the naked eye. Through a telescope, it looks rather like the Milky Way would look if viewed at a different angle.

Roughly how many light years is it from our galaxy to the centre of the Virgo Cluster?

The most distant objects that can be seen from earth using powerful telescopes are called **quasars**. *They are probably galaxies that give out far more light than ordinary galaxies.*

Try to find out something about quasars. You could:

● look up 'quasar' in a dictionary

● use an up-to-date book, for example from a library, to find how far it is to the most distant known quasar.

FINDING OUT ABOUT FOOD

Lots of labels

These labels come from different types of food.

Look at the labels. Use the information to make a table showing the contents of each food. You will need to decide what headings to use for your table.

1 Which substances are present in most of the foods?

2 Why do you think most of the labels show the nutritional information per 100 g of food?

Ten years ago, most food labels did not show nutritional information. Suggest some reasons why people now want to see nutritional information on food labels.

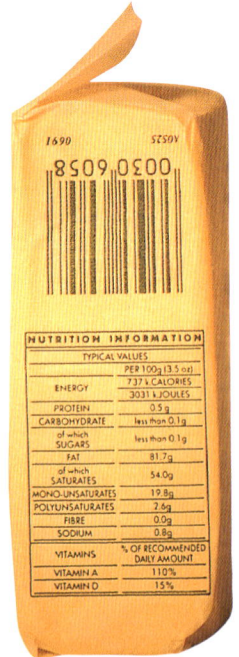

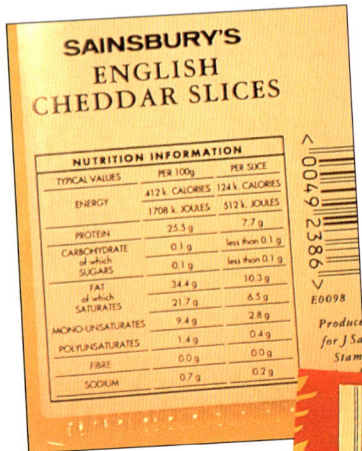

SEMI-SKIMMED MILK

NUTRITION INFORMATION
100 MILLILITRES OF THIS PRODUCT
TYPICALLY PROVIDES

Energy Value	203kJ
(Calories)	(48kcal)
3.4 grams of Protein	MEDIUM
4.9 grams of Carbohydrate	MEDIUM
1.7 grams of Fat	LOW

100 millilitres of this milk will typically provide the following proportions of the adult recommended daily amount.

Riboflavin (B$_2$)	11%
Vitamin B$_{12}$	20%
Calcium	24%

NUTRITION INFORMATION

TYPICAL VALUES

	PER 100g (3.5 oz)
ENERGY	737 k CALORIES
	3031 k JOULES
PROTEIN	0.5 g
CARBOHYDRATE	less than 0.1 g
of which SUGARS	less than 0.1 g
FAT	81.7g
of which SATURATES	54.0g
MONO-UNSATURATES	19.8g
POLYUNSATURATES	2.6g
FIBRE	0.0g
SODIUM	0.8g

VITAMINS	% OF RECOMMENDED DAILY AMOUNT
VITAMIN A	110%
VITAMIN D	15%

SAINSBURY'S ENGLISH CHEDDAR SLICES

NUTRITION INFORMATION

TYPICAL VALUES	PER 100g	PER SLICE
ENERGY	412 k CALORIES	124 k CALORIES
	1708 k JOULES	512 k JOULES
PROTEIN	25.5 g	7.7 g
CARBOHYDRATE	0.1 g	less than 0.1 g
of which SUGARS	0.1 g	less than 0.1 g
FAT	34.4 g	10.3 g
of which SATURATES	21.7 g	6.5 g
MONO-UNSATURATES	9.4 g	2.8 g
POLYUNSATURATES	1.4 g	0.4 g
FIBRE	0.0 g	0.0 g
SODIUM	0.7 g	0.2 g

E0098

Caramel CREAMY BAR

Ingredients:
Vegetable fat, Sweetened condensed skimmed milk, Lactose, Skimmed milk powder, Sugar, Brown sugar, Butter, Emulsifier (lecithin), Salt, Flavouring.

Nutrition Information	100g provides	Each bar provides
Energy	2275kJ/545kcal	686kJ/164 kcal
Protein	6.8g	2.1g
Carbohydrate	56.3g	16.9g
Fat	32.5g	9.8g

McVITIE'S

INGREDIENTS
FLOUR, VEGETABLE OIL AND HYDROGENATED VEGETABLE FAT AND ANIMAL FAT, SUGAR, WHOLEMEAL FLOUR, CULTURED SKIMMED MILK, PARTIALLY INVERTED SUGAR SYRUP, RAISING AGENTS (SODIUM BICARBONATE, TARTARIC ACID), SALT

NUTRITION INFORMATION

TYPICAL COMPOSITION	per biscuit	per 100g
ENERGY	309kJ 73kcal	2095kJ 499kcal
PROTEIN	1.0g	6.5g
CARBOHYDRATE	9.8g	67.0g
FAT	3.3g	22.1g

250 g e

Store in a cool dry place away from strong light
Made in Great Britain by McVitie's,
P.O. Box 63, York, YO1 1FS

ORANGE JUICE

	Per 100 ml
Energy	178 kJ/42 kcal
Fat	0
Protein	0.6 g
Carbohydrate	10.5 g
Vitamin C	30 mg

Bran Flakes

INGREDIENTS
WHEAT BRAN, SUGAR, MALT FLAVOURING, SALT, NIACIN, IRON, VITAMIN B$_6$, THIAMIN (B$_1$), RIBOFLAVIN (B$_2$), FOLIC ACID, VITAMIN D, VITAMIN B$_{12}$.

NUTRITION INFORMATION

		Per 100g	Per 40g Serving with 125ml of Semi-Skimmed Milk
ENERGY	kJ	1150	700*
	kcal	280	170
PROTEIN	g	14	10
CARBOHYDRATE	g	47	25
(of which sugars)	g	(18)	(14)
(starch)	g	(29)	(11)
FAT	g	3.5	3.5*
(of which saturates)	g	(0.6)	(1.5)
FIBRE	g	24	9.6
SODIUM	g	0.9	0.4
VITAMINS:			
NIACIN	mg	11.3	4.6
VITAMIN B$_6$	mg	1.3	0.6
RIBOFLAVIN (B$_2$)	mg	1.0	0.6
THIAMIN (B$_1$)	mg	0.8	0.4
FOLIC ACID	µg	188	80
VITAMIN D	µg	1.6	0.6
VITAMIN B$_{12}$	µg	1.3	1.0
IRON	mg	12	4.9
CALCIUM	mg	70	180
MAGNESIUM	mg	220	100
ZINC	mg	6.7	3.2

CREAMERY BUTTER

	Per 100 g
Energy	3032 kJ
Protein	0.5 g
Carbohydrate	trace
Fat	81.7 g
Sodium	0.8 g

NUTRITION
Sainsbury's Thick Sliced Wholemeal Bread is a good source of dietary fibre, which is the roughage in food needed for a healthy digestive system. It is also a good source of the B Vitamins, Thiamin and Niacin which help food to provide energy, and Iron, which is needed for healthy blood.

INGREDIENTS: WHOLEMEAL FLOUR, WATER, SALT, VEGETABLE FAT, YEAST, VINEGAR, WHEAT PROTEIN, SOYA FLOUR, EMULSIFIER: MONO- AND DIACETYLTARTARIC ACID ESTERS OF MONO- AND DIGLYCERIDES OF FATTY ACIDS; FLOUR IMPROVER: L-ASCORBIC ACID (VITAMIN C).

TYPICAL VALUES	PER 100 g (3½ oz)	PER SERVING (3 SLICES 126g)
ENERGY	215 k CALORIES 920 k JOULES	270 k CALORIES 1160 k JOULES
PROTEIN	10.3g	13.0g
CARBOHYDRATE AVAILABLE	40.2g	50.7g
TOTAL FAT	2.7g	3.4g
DIETARY FIBRE	8.4g	10.6g
ADDED SUGARS	0.3g	0.4g
ADDED SALT	1.2g	1.5g

VITAMINS/MINERALS	% OF RECOMMENDED DAILY AMOUNT	
THIAMIN (VITAMIN B1)	25%	32%
NIACIN	22%	28%
IRON	22%	28%

For BEST BEFORE date see bag closure. If freezing, place in deep freeze on day of purchase, use within three months.

STORE IN A COOL DRY PLACE

Wholemeal Bread 800 gram
Flour used: Wholemeal flour consisting of approximately 85% Endosperm, 12% Bran, 3% Wheatgerm.

Produced in UK for J Sainsbury plc
Stamford Street, London SE1 9LL

Why do we need food?

You often hear people talking about food …

3 Look carefully at each of the statements about food.

● Which do you agree with?

● Which do you disagree with?

● Which are you not sure about?

4 Why do you think people need food?

Most people get enough vitamins and minerals in their diet.

Chocolate gives you lots of energy.

Milk is a complete food because it contains protein, fat, carbohydrate and vitamins.

Salt is bad for you.

Artificial preservatives and colourings should not be added to food.

Foods which contain fat are bad for you.

You need protein to help you grow.

Brown bread is better for you than white bread.

You need to eat meat to have a balanced diet.

Foods which contain lots of carbohydrate are good energy stores.

FOOD FACTS

Nutrients

You may have tested foods for three types of nutrient – **carbohydrates**, **fats** and **protein**. There are two other important groups of chemicals in food – **vitamins** and **minerals**.
A nutrient is a chemical that nourishes us. This page shows how the five important groups of nutrient do this.

Fats

Fats are high-energy nutrients that are stored in the body under the skin. Fat stores help to keep you warm, but too much stored fat increases the risk of certain diseases.

Carbohydrates

There are three types of carbo-hydrates: starches, sugars and fibre. Starches and sugars provide energy, though too much sugar can lead to tooth decay. Fibre is needed for a healthy digestive system.

Proteins

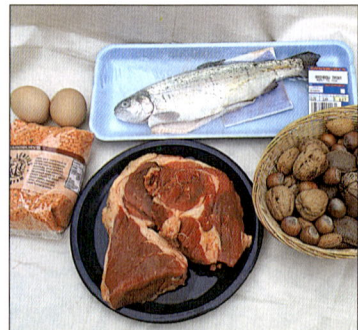

Proteins are needed to help you grow and repair and replace cells in your body.

Vitamins

Some important vitamins are shown in the table:

Vitamin	Needed for	Found in
A	Good eyesight	Dairy products, liver, carrots
B group	Muscle coordination	Eggs, liver, wholemeal products
C	Protection against disease	Citrus fruits, potatoes
D	Teeth and bones	Dairy products, also made in skin cells in sunlight

Small quantities of each vitamin are vital for good health.

Minerals

Small quantities of various minerals are also vital for good health.

Two important groups of minerals are:
• calcium compounds, which are needed for healthy teeth and bones. Calcium compounds are found in dairy products.
• iron compounds, which are needed for healthy red blood cells. Iron compounds are found in meat and leafy green vegetables.

What's for breakfast?

For breakfast, Gary has a 50 g bowl of bran flakes with 125 cm³ of semi-skimmed milk. Danuta has two slices of wholemeal toast with 25 g of butter, and 140 cm³ glass of orange juice.

Use the information on page 36 and the table below to find out which breakfast contains the most:

- protein
- fat
- carbohydrate
- vitamin A
- vitamin D
- iron compounds.

Nutrient	Bran flakes (per 100 g)	Semi-skimmed milk (per 125 cm³)	Wholemeal bread (per slice)	Butter (per 100 g)	Orange juice (per 100 ml)
Vitamin A (µg)	0	200	0	3500	0
Vitamin B1 (mg)	1.0	0.1	0.1	0	0
Vitamin B2 (mg)	1.3	0.2	0.05	0	0
Vitamin B12 (mg)	1.7	0.5	1.3	0	0
Vitamin C (mg)	25	2.0	0	0	30
Vitamin D (µg)	2.1	0.2	0	39	0
Calcium compounds (mg)	50	155	10	15	0
Iron compounds (mg)	20	0.1	1.2	0	0

Additives

*Other chemicals may be added to foods by food manufacturers and processors. They may be added to make the food look or taste better, or to help preserve the food. Many of these chemicals are identified by their **E-number** which shows that they are authorized by the European Commission. The table shows some food additives and their functions.*

Food additive	Function
E100 – E180	Colourings, added to make food look more attractive
E200 – E290	Preservatives, added to stop bacteria growing on the food
E300 – E321	Antioxidants, added to stop the food reacting with oxygen in the air
E322 – E494	Stabilizers, added to prevent chemical or physical changes taking place in the food
Sweeteners	Added to sweeten food – most do not have E-numbers
Flavourings	Added to improve flavour – many do not have E-numbers, but the common flavouring monosodium glutamate has the number E621

Lunchtime snack

Anne's mum takes sandwiches, a packet of soup and a yoghurt to work for her lunch. She notices on the labels that her soup contains E471 and E472 additives, and her yoghurt contains additive E202.

1 What types of additives have been added to the soup and yoghurt? Why have they been added?

PRESERVING FOOD

'Going off'

A problem with food is that it 'goes off'. This means that it begins to decompose, because microbes are growing in it. Microbes are tiny living organisms such as bacteria and fungi. If food is left, microbes can multiply rapidly in it.

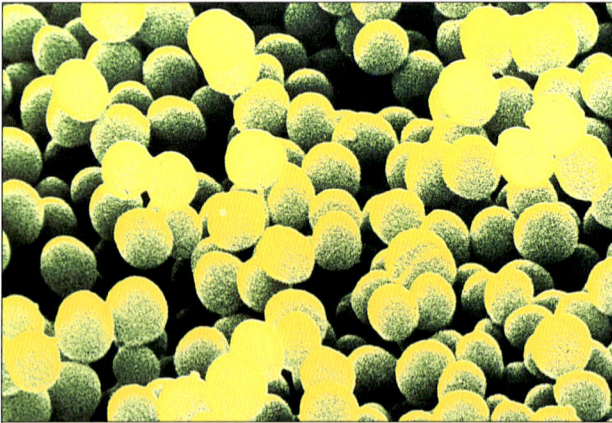

Salmonella (magnified 6864 times) are harmful bacteria which can grow in meat, soups, milk and eggs. Thorough cooking kills them and so prevents you becoming ill.

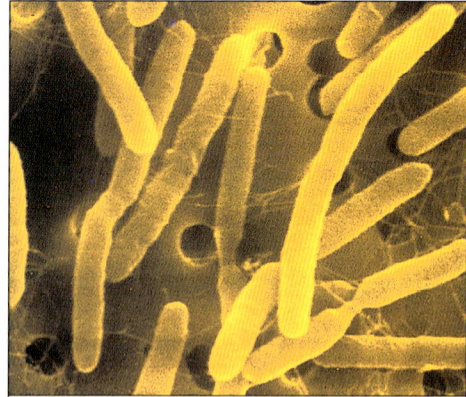

Staphylococci (magnified 9100 times) are bacteria which grow in food and produce harmful toxins (poisonous chemicals). Although the bacteria are killed by cooking, the toxins can still make you ill.

If you eat food which has gone off then the microbes, or substances made by the microbes, can make you ill. You get food poisoning.

Why preserve food?

It would be a good idea to eat nothing but fresh food all the time, but there are problems:

Some foods are seasonal. It would be very boring to eat lots of peas in the summer and none for the rest of the year.

Some foods have to be transported long distances. This takes a long time and the food is not as fresh when it arrives as when it left.

Sometimes it is more interesting or more convenient to have preserved food.

Smoking food preserves it and gives it a distinctive taste.

Make a table showing foods that are preserved for each of these reasons. Try to think of at least two foods in each column of your table.

Ways of preserving food

Sultanas are grapes which have been dried in the sun. Drying takes away the water needed by the microbes.

In order to preserve food, you have to either kill all the microbes in the food or stop them multiplying quickly.

1 Why do you think it is important to know which method has been used to preserve a particular food – whether all the microbes have been killed or not?

For thousands of years drying, pickling and salting have been traditional ways of preserving foods.

Bacon is pork which has been soaked in a concentrated solution of salt. The salt stops microbes growing.

These limes have been pickled in vinegar. Microbes do not grow well in acidic conditions.

Jam is made by boiling fruit with a lot of sugar. Microbes do not grow well in a concentrated sugar solution.

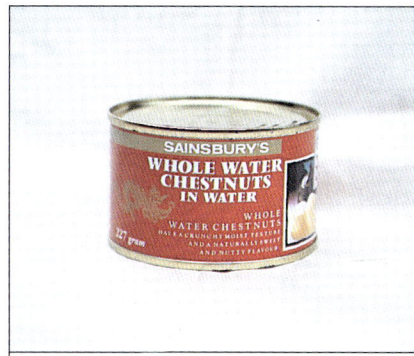

Food is cooked and then sealed in cans. The cooking kills the microbes. Sealing it in cans stops any more microbes getting in.

Irradiation of food by gamma rays from a radioactive material such as cobalt-60 will kill microbes. The food can be packaged before irradiation as the radiation passes through the packaging.

Pre-prepared meals are quickly frozen by pouring liquid nitrogen over them. This freezes the water needed by the microbes and slows down all chemical changes.

Using the information on this page, make a table which summarizes the methods of preserving food. Include enough information to remind you what is done in each method, how it works and what sorts of foods it is used for.

SAFETY FIRST

Accidents will happen

Whatever you are doing, it is always possible for an accident to happen. Many accidents are slight, but some are serious. Each year, large numbers of people die as a result of accidents.

The pictures on these two pages show people enjoying various activities.

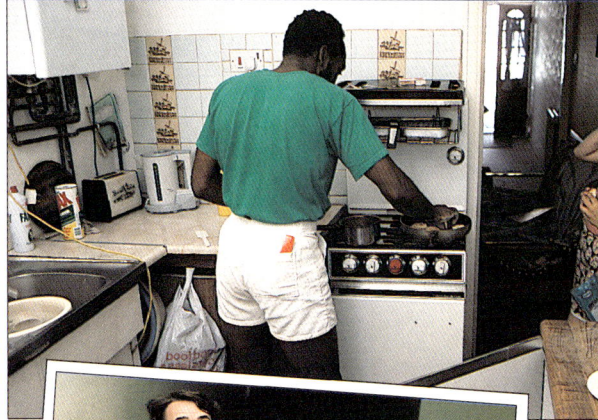

Discuss which activities you think could most easily lead to a serious accident. List the activities in order of how dangerous you think they are.

Some of the activities are part of most people's daily life; others are things a few people chose to do.

Discuss which activities you think involve the largest number of people.

Discuss which activities you think might lead to the largest number of serious accidents. List the activities in order, with the one you think leads to the largest number of serious accidents at the top.

Better safe than sorry

In some activities, there are things you can do to make accidents less serious if they do happen (for example, wearing a helmet when riding a horse or motorbike). Some accidents can be prevented (for example, by putting a guard in front of the fire).

Choose *one* activity and describe how you could make it as safe as possible.

HOW FAST? HOW FAR?

▲ British Rail's 225 train is so called because it can travel at 225 km/h.

▨ Find out the name, and the speed, of the world's fastest train.

A world class sprinter can run 100 m in 10 s. ▶

1 What is his average speed in m/s?

Record speeds

The speed limit in towns is normally 30 m.p.h.

▨ Find out the normal speed limits for:

● single carriageway roads outside built-up areas

● dual carriageways

● motorways.

◀ A marathon runner runs 26.2 miles in 2½ hours.

26.2 miles = 42 195 m
2½ hours = 9000 s

2 What is her average speed in m/s?

3 Why is the average speed of a sprinter greater than that of a marathon runner?

Find out the world record times for:

● the 100 m sprint   ● the marathon.

In the Derby, horses run 2423 m in 180 s.

4 How does their average speed compare with that of a human runner? ▼

◀ Racing pigeons can fly 200 miles in 4 hours.

5 What is their average speed in miles per hour?

On the road

Aberdeen	652	787	554	943	208	679	531	816	1069	628	872	370	509
	Birmingham	161	153	285	452	232	142	171	428	69	200	470	206
		Cardiff	314	351	587	343	261	237	362	167	185	605	367
			Doncaster	364	346	267	130	262	578	158	320	399	53
405				Dover	718	533	426	114	554	352	220	748	301
489	100				Edinburgh	480	331	608	869	420	665	200	306
344	95	195				Holyhead	148	402	658	162	425	497	150
586	177	218	226				Liverpool	325	550	93	341	349	636
129	281	365	215	446				London	439	240	130	636	315
422	144	213	166	331	298				Penzance	443	328	887	439
330	88	162	81	265	206	92				Shrewsbury	262	438	214
507	106	147	163	71	378	250	202				Southampton	682	380
664	266	225	359	344	540	409	342	273				Stranraer	352
390	43	104	98	219	261	101	58	149	275				York
542	125	115	199	137	413	264	212	81	204	163			
230	292	376	248	465	124	309	217	395	551	272	424		
316	128	228	33	274	187	190	93	196	395	133	236	219	

distance in miles

Journey planners like this are included in many road atlases. They are used to find distances between large towns. For example, from Cardiff to Stranraer is 376 miles or 605 kilometres.

Use an atlas to find the towns in this journey planner.

Find the distances in miles between:

● London and York   ● Liverpool and Edinburgh   ● Penzance and Dover.

Calculate the average speed in miles per hour, for each of these journeys:

● London to York by train in 2 hours

● Liverpool to Edinburgh by coach in 5 hours

● Penzance to Dover by car in 8½ hours.

If a car travels at an average speed of 30 miles per hour, how far does it travel in:

● 2 hours   ● 4 hours?

Copy and complete this word equation so that it tells you how to calculate distances if you know the time taken and the average speed:

Distance travelled =

6 If a coach travels with an average speed of 50 miles per hour, how long would it take to go:

● from Birmingham to Cardiff   ● from Holyhead to London?

Copy and complete this word equation so that it tells you how you how to calculate the time for a journey if you know the distance and the average speed:

Time taken =

SEEN TO BE SAFE

Local boy in bike accident

Mike Duncan, aged 14, was knocked off his bicycle yesterday at the corner of Salters' Square. Mike's mother, a leader of the residents' campaign for safer streets, said:
'Luckily he was not badly hurt. That corner's a death trap. Something should be done about it.'

The car driver said:
'I didn't see him. It was getting dark and he was dressed in dark clothes with no lights or reflectors on his bike. It's not fair always to blame the motorist.'

Be safe – be seen

Cyclists and pedestrians can make themselves easier to see.

- List as many ways of doing this as you can think of.

1 Which ways give out their own light? Which rely on light from street lights and headlamps to make them show up?

- Discuss how you could test some of the things you have listed. Before you carry out your tests, look carefully at these pictures.

A street in daylight …

… and at night, lit by yellow sodium street lights.

- Look at the things that are in both pictures. Describe carefully any differences in their appearance.

- Discuss what sort of lighting you should use in your tests. Then test different ways of making people more visible at night.

- Write a report of your tests. Your report should say which methods you recommend to cyclists and pedestrians. As well as visibility, there may be other factors, such as cost, that you need to think about.

Now you see it...

You will have seen that things appear to change colour when lit by yellow street lamps. The pictures on this page are in six different colours. Use them to explore the changes produced by coloured lights.

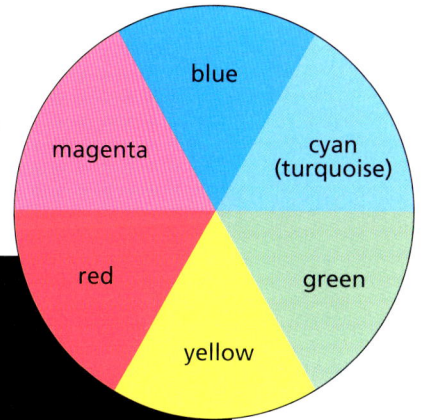

You will need to use different coloured lights. Try to carry out one or more of these activities:

Predict the colours that you will see when you shine coloured light onto this page.

Test your prediction.

Describe carefully the colours that you see when you shine coloured light onto the page.

Work with a partner. Use a large sheet of paper to cover the book so that only one picture is visible and shine coloured light onto it. Get your partner to decide which picture it is.

2 When choosing paint or fabric, why is it a good idea to use natural daylight?

47

PLANNING TO BE SAFER

The people living around Salters' Square are worried about the number of road accidents in their area. They want the council to make the area safer.

The council have collected information about all the accidents that took place in one year.

Look at this map, and try to predict where the danger spots might be. You might want to think about possible dangers to:

- young children
- old people
- cyclists
- car drivers.

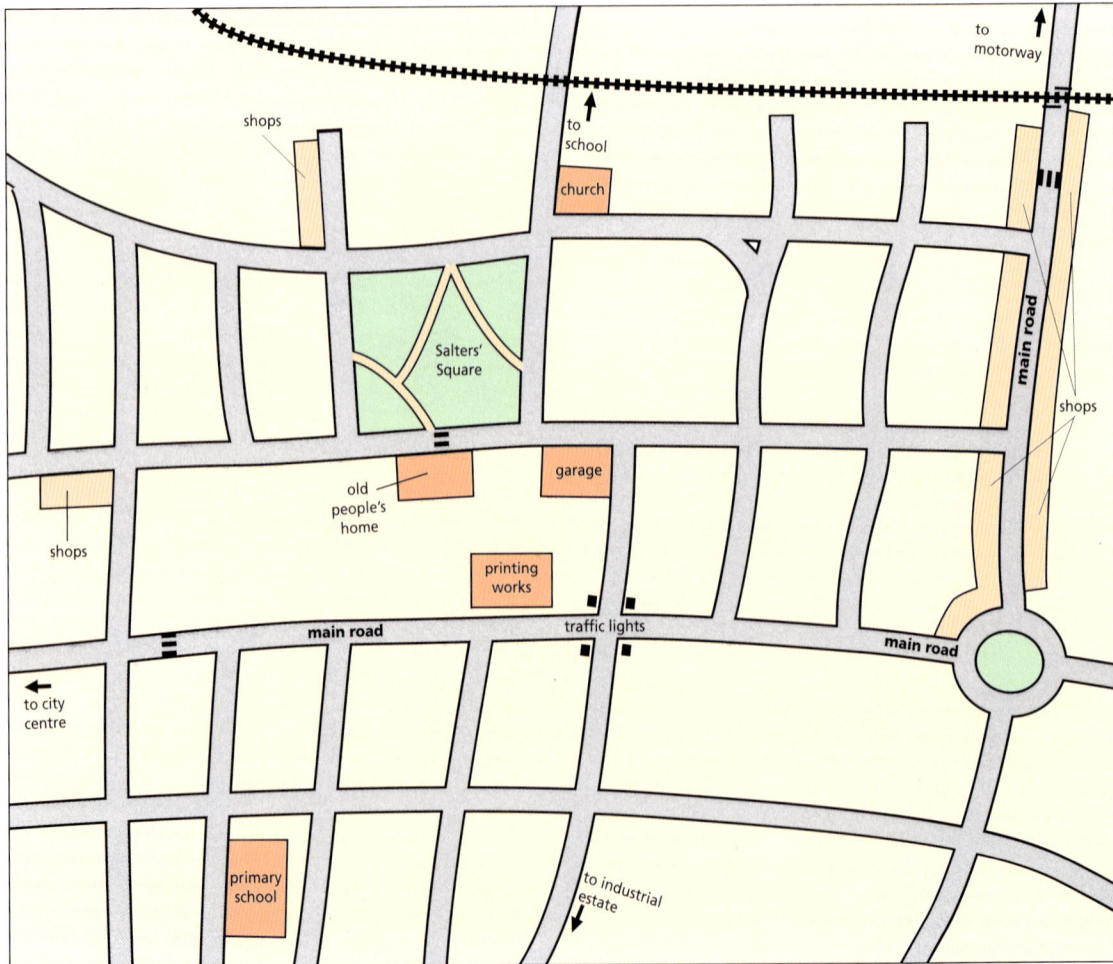

Map showing: to motorway, shops, to school, church, main road, Salters' Square, shops, old people's home, garage, printing works, shops, main road, traffic lights, main road, to city centre, primary school, to industrial estate.

Would it be enough for the council just to record *where* each accident took place? What other information do you think they should collect? Discuss your ideas.

The council plan to spend up to £50 000 on making the area safer. People have suggested various things they could do.

Look at the suggestions on the next page and discuss the advantages and disadvantages of each.

Make a note of any other things that you think the council could do.

Installing roundabouts at junctions, £35 000 each

Making the square 'pedestrians only' – putting up barriers, £5000

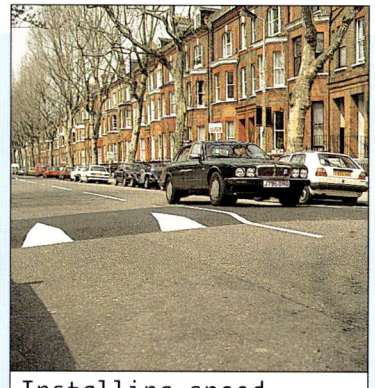

Installing speed-bumps to slow down the traffic, £500 each

Installing traffic lights at junctions, £25 000 per junction

Running an education campaign in local schools, £2000

Banning lorries from side streets, £3000

Banning non-residents from driving on the side streets, £3000

Installing a zebra crossing, £8000

Employing a school crossing warden, £2000 per year

Making the speed limit 20 m.p.h. – putting up new signs, £3000

Running a poster campaign in the town, £2000

The council are to hold a public meeting to discuss what to do. Different people will put forward their points of view.

Discuss what you would want the council to do if you were:

- a parent with young children
- a cyclist
- a shopkeeper
- the manager of a firm that does road works for the council
- the council treasurer

- a resident in the old people's home
- a school crossing warden
- a car driver who lives in Salters' Square
- a car driver living out of town who drives through Salters' Square every day.

BRINGING HOME THE BABY

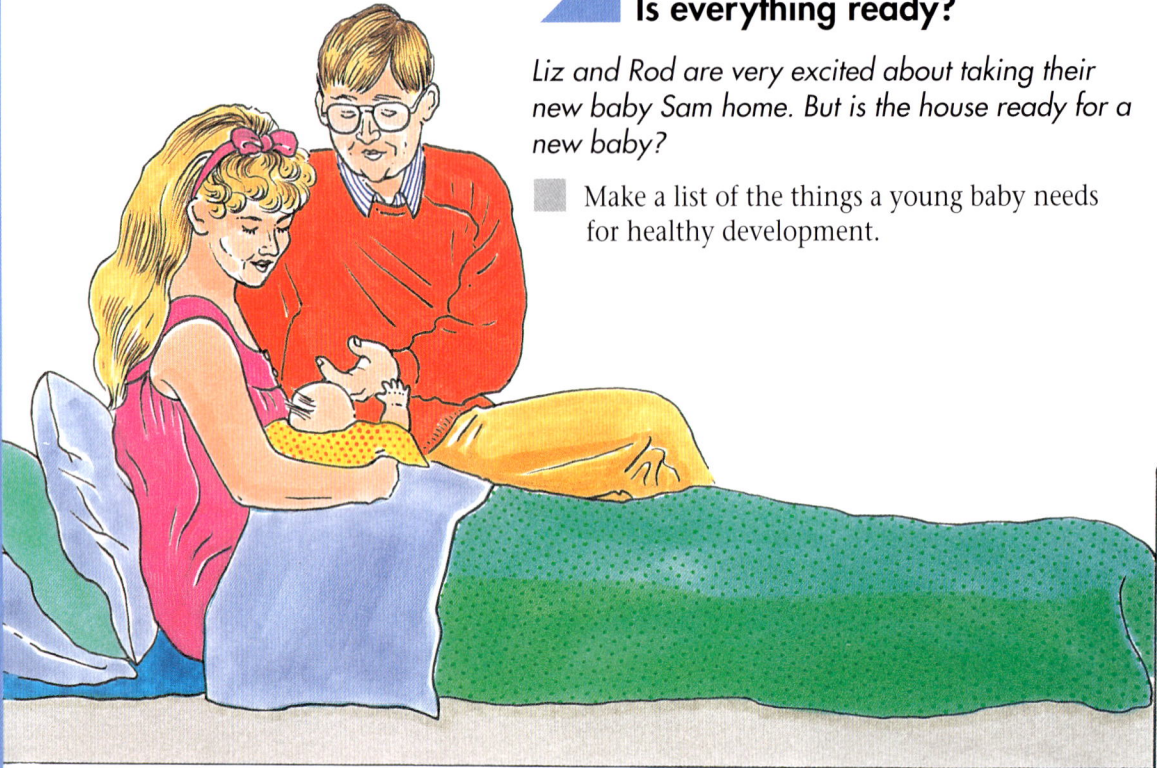

Is everything ready?

Liz and Rod are very excited about taking their new baby Sam home. But is the house ready for a new baby?

Make a list of the things a young baby needs for healthy development.

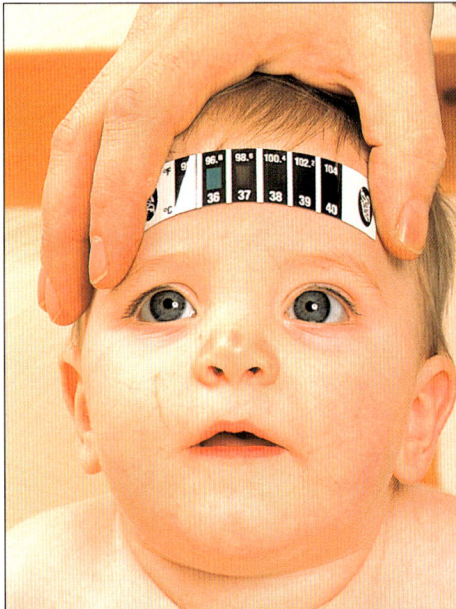

In hospital, Sam's temperature was measured regularly using a mercury thermometer. At home, Sam's parents measure his temperature using a colour-change strip thermometer, like this one.

Warm and cosy

Normal body temperature is about 37 °C. Babies have a temperature slightly higher than this.

Our bodies have a control system which works to keep our temperature constant. In young babies this system does not work yet, so babies cannot control their body temperature.

It is very dangerous to let babies get too cold or too hot. If their body temperature falls, they cannot warm themselves up, and can suffer from hypothermia. This dangerous condition needs urgent medical help.

Warmly dressed and well fed babies will keep warm as long as the room temperature stays above about 20 °C.

1 If a sleeping baby has become cold, why does adding extra blankets not help?

2 What advantages does the colour-change thermometer have over a mercury thermometer?

Nice and clean

Even the cleanest looking kitchen is covered in germs. Most are harmless because our bodies build up a resistance to them, but a young baby has very little resistance. A baby's bottle and feeding dish provide a perfect environment for germs to grow. If the dishes are not sterilized, the baby may get a serious infection, causing vomiting and diarrhoea.

In this picture Rod is sterilizing a rattle with a special chemical sterilizing solution.

3 Why do germs grow well on babies' bottles and feeding dishes?

Better safe than sorry

Babies are naturally curious and want to investigate everything. When Sam starts to move around, his parents will have to make sure that the house is as safe as possible.

Make a list of as many possible dangers as you can see in this kitchen. How could each of these dangers be avoided?

BABY GROWTH

A visit to the clinic

Liz takes Sam to the child heath clinic every week. The health visitor checks that Sam is making good progress and answers any questions that might be worrying Liz.

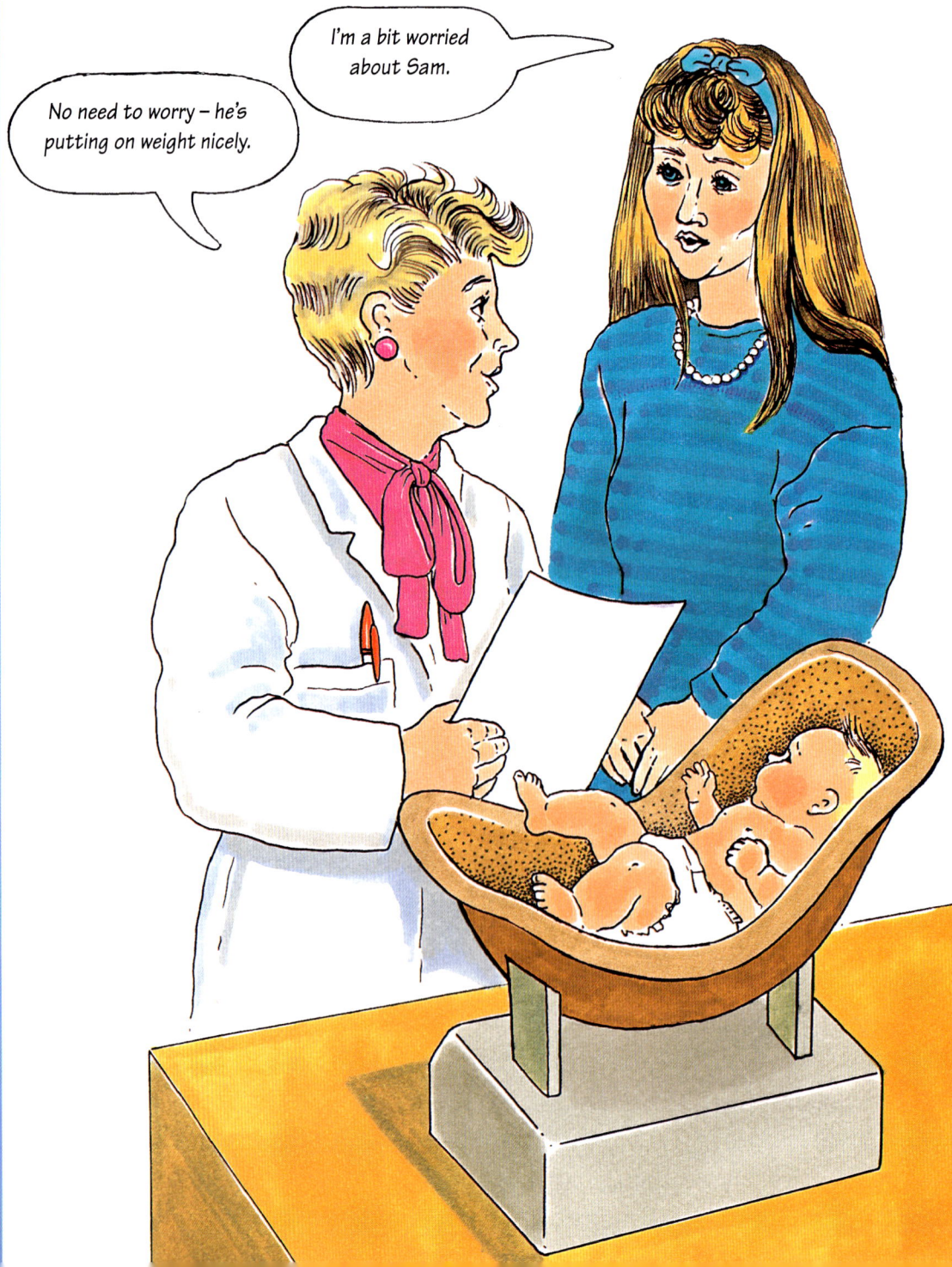

I'm a bit worried about Sam.

No need to worry – he's putting on weight nicely.

Changes in mass

A useful way to check Sam's progress is to weigh him regularly.

The health visitor plots his mass on a chart. The chart has three reference lines drawn on it. A healthy baby's mass is expected to fall between lines A and B. Line C is the mass change that an average baby would show.

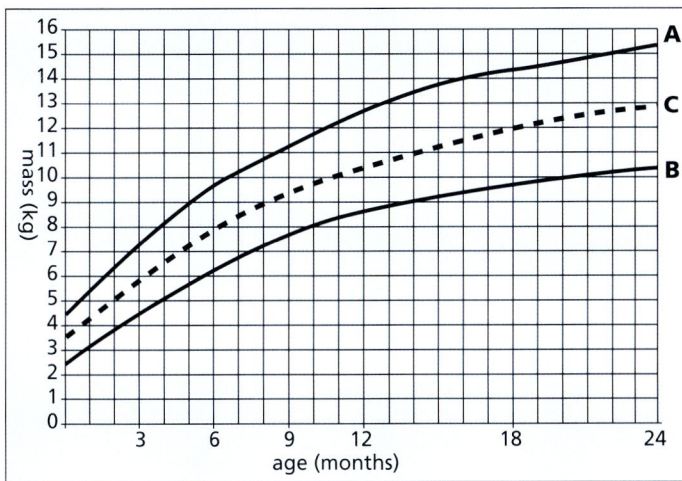

Age (months)	Mass (kg)	
	Sam	Mary
0	4.2	3.0
1	4.6	3.8
2	5.1	4.3
3	6.4	5.2
4	6.8	6.0
5	6.8	6.5
6	7.8	6.1
7	8.2	6.2
8	9.5	6.4
9	10.0	6.9
10	10.4	7.3
11	10.7	7.7
12	11.9	8.1

This activity shows how the mass of two babies changed over their first year.

- Use the table at the top of the page to plot a graph of each baby's gain in mass.

These notes are taken from the clinic's files. ▶

- Compare the notes with your graphs.

1 Whose file do you think these notes are taken from, Sam's or Mary's? Explain your answer.

Baby was breastfed until six months old. Seemed unhappy, mother started to give solids and powdered milk.
Baby liked this even less and was very unhappy.
20th June
Saw doctor. Suspects baby has malabsorption syndrome (cannot absorb cereals properly).
Put on a special diet - no wheat flour or cereal.

Feeding the baby

Like this mother, Liz is breastfeeding Sam. She is having some problems and wants to ask the nurse about bottle feeding.

- Discuss what you think are the advantages and disadvantages of breast and bottle feeding.

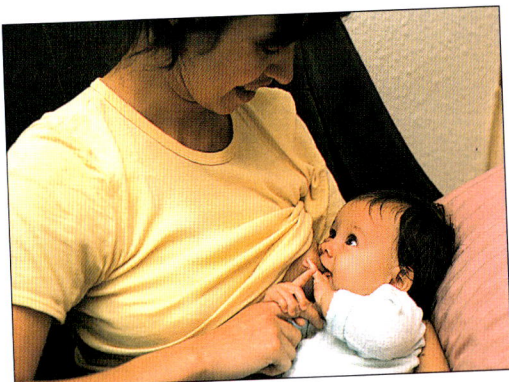

LEARNING THROUGH PLAY

A learning experience

Barbara is doing two weeks' work experience in a nursery. She wants to find out what being a nursery nurse is like. While she is there Barbara has to keep a daily diary of her experiences.

Friday

I am amazed how much Ashley has learned in the last two weeks. He can communicate much more and can get around really well. I have to be on my toes!

Make a list of the things a baby learns in the first two years. Use pages 56–7 to help you.

Are some toys better than others?

Barbara has an assignment to do which is linked with her work experience.

Work Experience Assignment

To help them learn, babies need stimulation. Toys are a good way of stimulating children. Toys help children practise new skills such as grasping and sorting.

Your task

You are to submit a design for a new educational toy.

Your plans should include:
- a clear diagram of the toy
- the age group for which the toy is designed
- the skills to be developed during play
- the materials to be used
- any special safety features.

What makes a good toy?

Use pages 56–7 to help you list the properties you think a good toy should have for babies of different ages. Do this for babies of one month, then three months, six months, etc. up to two years.

Age of baby	Properties of a good toy
1 month	Colourful Moves slowly where baby can see

F *Hammer and peg set*
6 mth–2 yr
Knock the pegs through. Excellent value.
£9.99 Ref 2.11

G *Stack 'a' ring*
6 mth–36 mth
6 brightly coloured rings. Stack them or squeeze them.
£3.25 Ref 2.22

F

G

Look carefully at this section from a toy catalogue.

1 Do you think the toys are right for the age recommended by the maker? If you disagree, say why, and suggest which age the toy is suitable for.

Designer toys

Now have a go at Barbara's assignment and design your own toy.
Don't forget the list of things which you must include in your plans.

HOW BABIES DEVELOP

1 month

Grasps finger

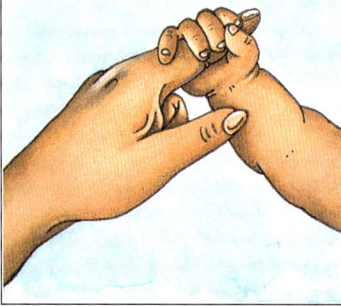

Eyes follow a moving ball

Stops whimpering to listen, turns head

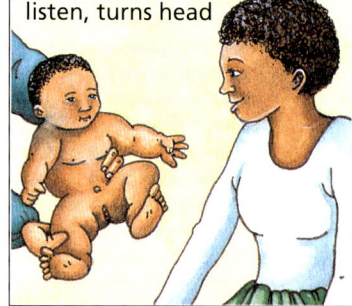

3 months

Turns to nearby voice

Follows a moving ball in vertical plane

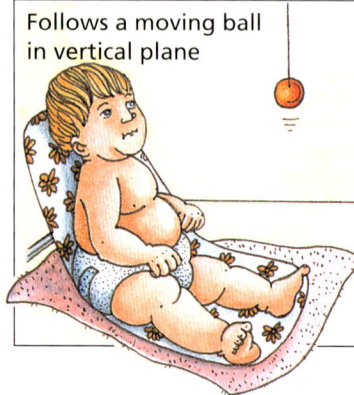

Holds toy but cannot look at it

6 months

Turns to quiet sounds at ear level

Grasps toy with both hands

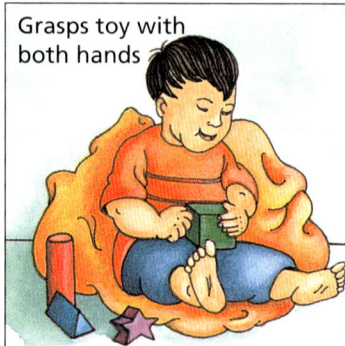

Watches a moving ball at about 2 metres

9 months

Looks at and feels the shape of objects

Lifts block but cannot place down

Grasps toy by handle and shakes

1 year

Plays pat-a-cake
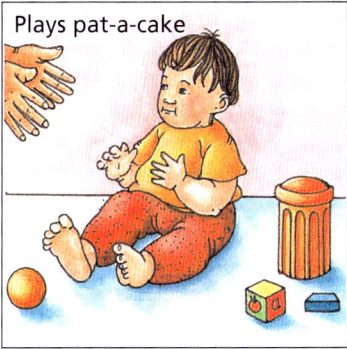

Walks with one hand held

Learns how to use simple everyday objects

15 months

Grasps crayon and scribbles lines
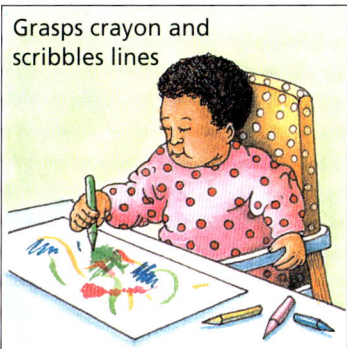

Pushes large wheeled toy on level

Builds tower of two blocks
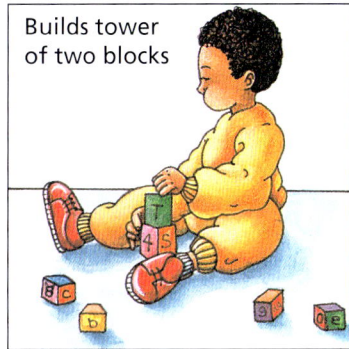

18 months

Pushes and pulls wheeled toy

Walks well carrying toy

Enjoys picture books
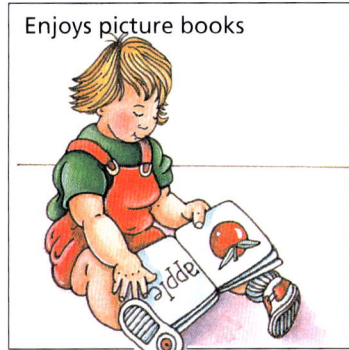

2 years

Builds a tower of six or seven bricks
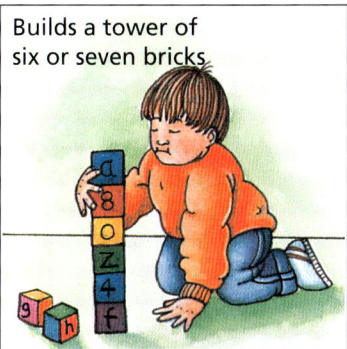

Engages in simple pretend play

Holds pencil and scribbles
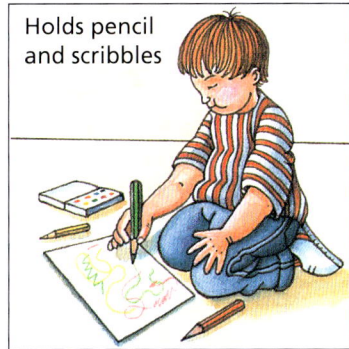

GROW YOUR BONE

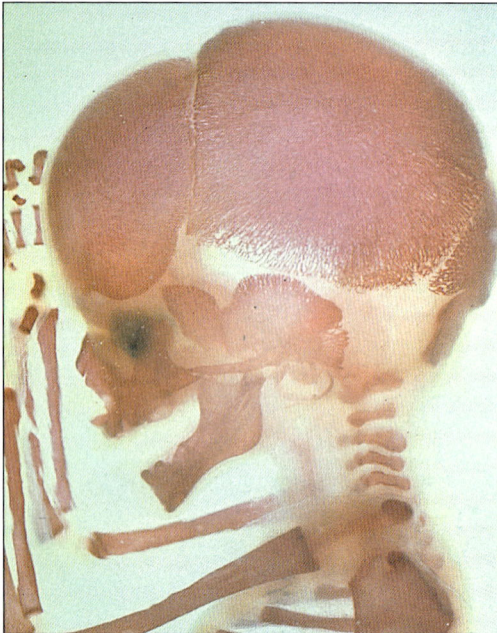

How bones begin

Bones form at an early stage in a baby's development. In this picture of an unborn baby the humerus (a bone between the shoulder and elbow) is only about 3 millimetres long. By the time the baby is 18 years old the bone will be about 100 times larger.

In fact, an unborn baby's bones are not bones at all! They are the same shape as bones but are made from a rubbery material called **cartilage**.

Estimate the size of an adult humerus.

How bones grow

As the baby's humerus grows, three areas begin to change into bone.

*Gradually most of the cartilage becomes bone, except two areas called **growth plates**.*

These plates of cartilage continue to grow. As new cartilage forms and turns to bone, the bone lengthens.

When the bone reaches its final length, the cartilage fuses with the bone and stops growing.

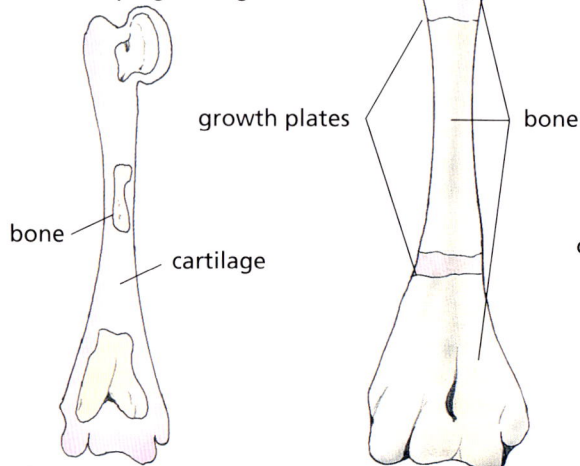

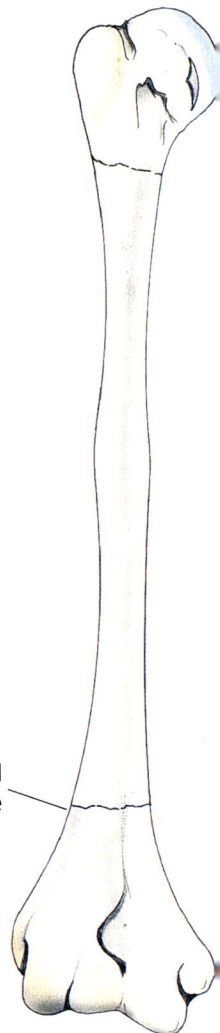

bone

cartilage

growth plates

bone

fused cartilage

Bendy bones

Young children's bones are quite soft and flexible. They harden gradually as the child grows. A good diet is important for a child's bones to develop and harden. It is important to eat enough calcium and vitamins A, C and D.

Explain why particular care should be taken when buying and fitting young children's shoes.

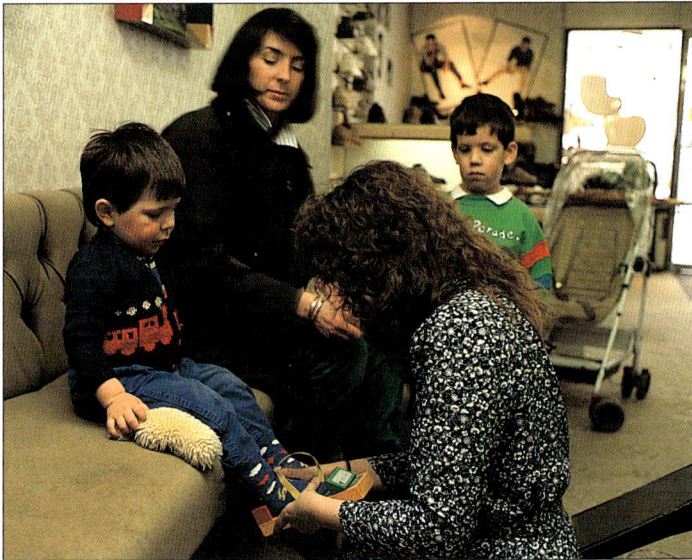

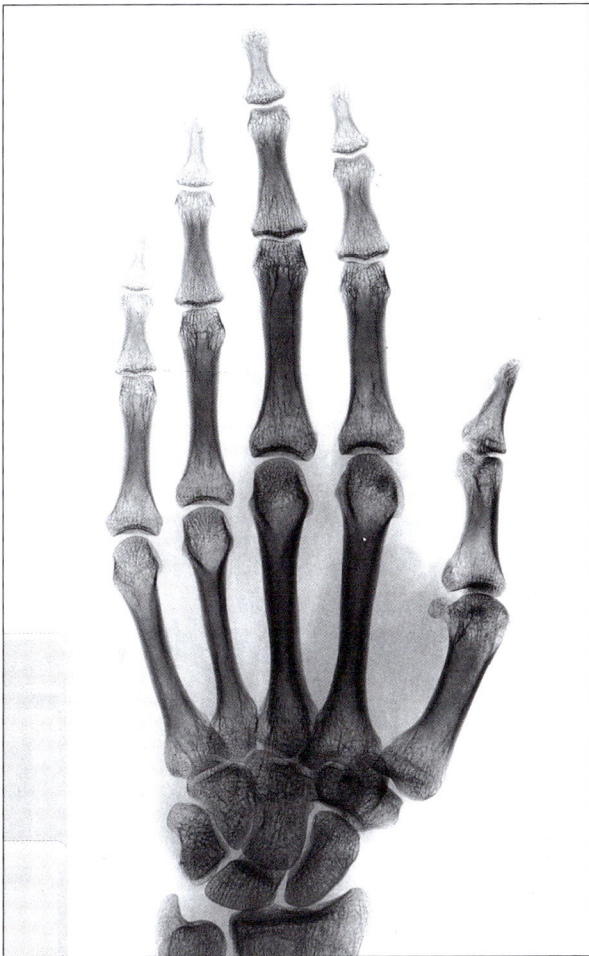

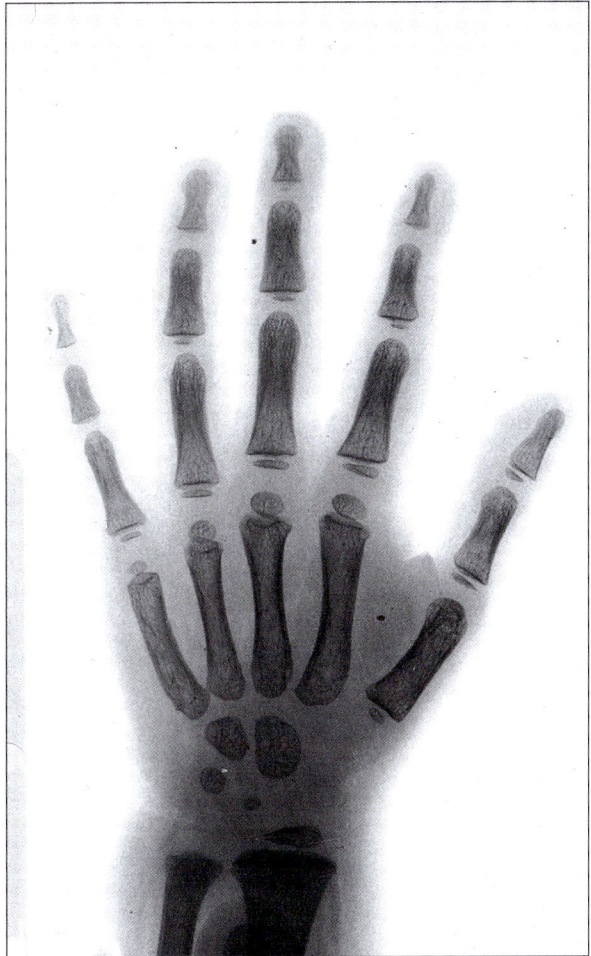

These photographs show the X–rays of a child's hand and an adult's hand.

1 Which is which? How can you tell?

AT HOME WITH MATERIALS

Sorting out materials

We are surrounded by things that people have made. When designing each object, somebody had to choose which materials to use.

In this unit you will learn about metals and other materials – about how materials are made and some of the characteristics that make them useful.

Materials in the kitchen

Many of the things in this kitchen are made from metal, wood, ceramic (pottery) or plastic.

Make a table like this:

Metal	Wood	Ceramic	Plastic

Under each heading, list at least three things in the kitchen made from that material.

A materials survey

Choose one particular type of 'made' object (such as sports equipment), or look at objects in one room at school or at home.

Decide what each object is made from.

Display the results of your survey to show which things are made from metal, wood, ceramic, plastic or other materials.

Materials old ...

1 Which type of material (metal, wood, ceramic or plastic) do you think was first used by early human beings? Why do you think this?

Use library books to find out about materials used to make equipment for preparing and cooking food:

● a few hundred years ago

● many thousands of years ago.

... and new

Many things we use today are made from plastic, but the first plastics were invented only about 100 years ago.

List some everyday objects that are made from plastic, and discuss these questions for each object.

● Could it be made from any other material?

● If so, what might it have been made from before plastics were invented?

Try to think of reasons why plastics are used so widely today. Some reasons might involve how plastics and other materials behave. There might also be other reasons, such as cost.

Compare your ideas with those of other students.

CERAMICS

These wine jars were made in Greece about 2500 years ago.

Ceramic materials have been used for thousands of years, for example to make containers and sculptures. Brick is also a ceramic material.

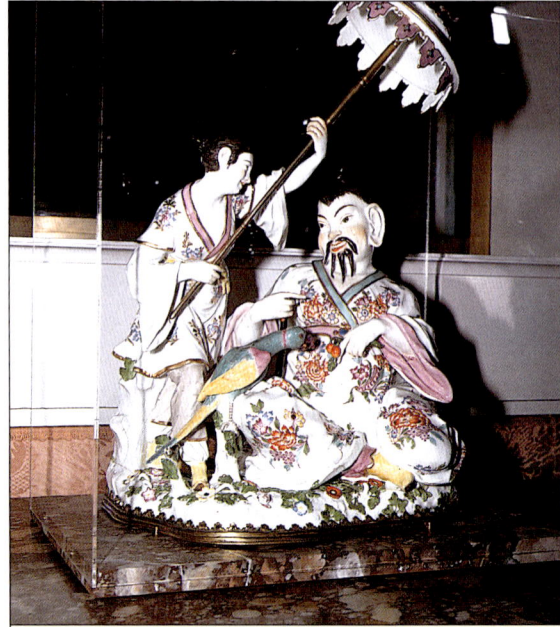

This Japanese figure was made in 1745.

Nowadays special ceramics are used in car engines...

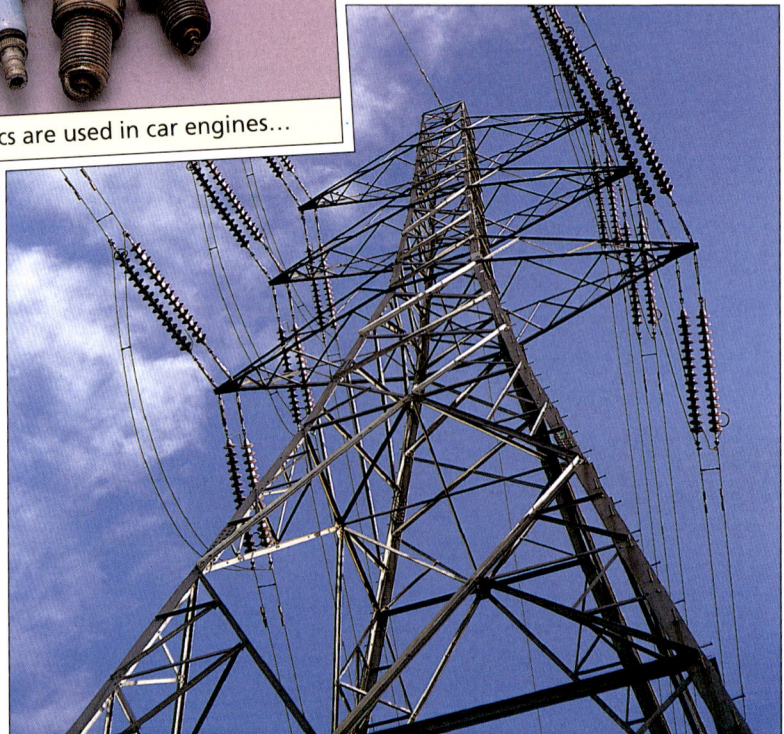

... and on pylons that support electrical cables.

62

Making ceramic materials

◀ The simplest ceramics are made from clay dug from the ground. The soft, sticky clay is shaped and allowed to dry. It may be decorated or dipped in **glaze**. ▼

▲ It is then **fired** in a kiln (a very hot oven).

Firing makes the clay into a very hard material – a ceramic material. If it is glazed it will be coated in a very thin layer of glass that makes it shiny and stops water soaking into it.

The suitability of ceramics

Use your own tests and observations to decide which characteristics of ceramics make them good materials for:

● containers for liquids

● ornaments

● parts for car engines

● false teeth

● cooker hobs

● 'spacers' to separate electrical cables from pylons.

What do you think might be a disadvantage of ceramics for each of these uses?

Discuss your ideas.

MANY METALS

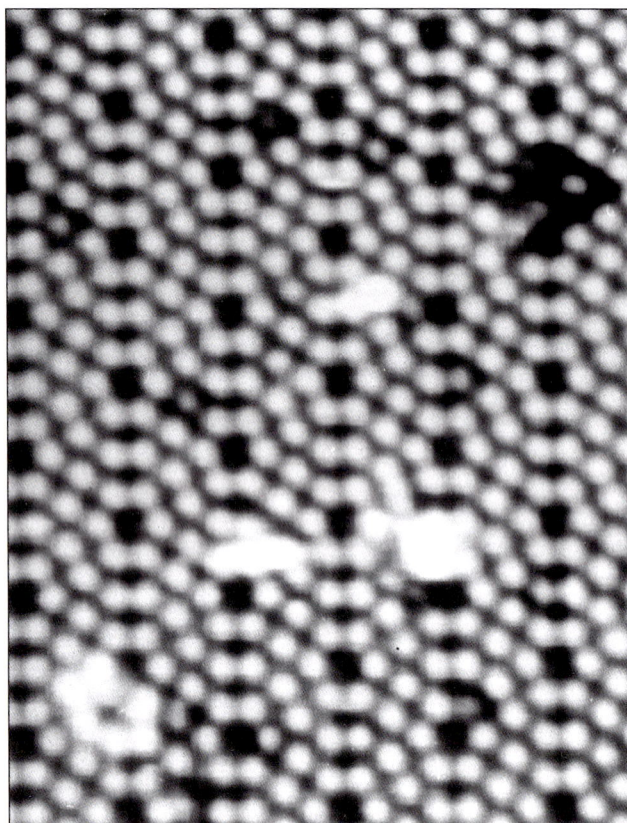

Pure metals

Pure metals are examples of the simplest type of substance. They are **elements**. An element is a substance that cannot be split up into any simpler substance. All atoms of an element are of the same type.

Elements can be represented by **symbols**. The same symbols are used all over the world.

This picture shows the surface of silicon (a non-metal element). It was made with a very powerful microscope, called a scanning tunnelling electron microscope, and shows the individual silicon atoms.

This table gives information about some common metals.

Metal	Symbol	Approximate cost per kilogram (£)	World annual production (thousands of tonnes)	Density (g/cm³)	Melting point (°C)	Conductivity of heat (1 = best conductor, 9 = worst conductor)	Conductivity of electricity (1 = best conductor, 9 = worst conductor)
Aluminium	Al	0.81	7900	2.7	660	4	4
Copper	Cu	0.92	4750	8.9	1083	2	2
Gold	Au	6428	2	19.3	1063	3	3
Iron	Fe	0.13	301 430	7.9	1535	8	7
Lead	Pb	0.38	2670	11.3	327	9	9
Nickel	Ni	3.44	370	8.9	1453	7	6
Silver	Ag	2178	8	10.5	961	1	1
Tin	Sn	9.18	200	7.3	232	6	8
Zinc	Zn	0.66	3970	7.1	420	5	5

Which metal?

The ideal saucepan

Saucepans need to be made from a material that conducts heat, so that the food can be heated inside them. But the best conductor is not necessarily the most suitable material.

1 Which metal in the table is the best heat conductor?

Suggest as many reasons as you can why the best conductor is not used for saucepans.

2 Which metals in the table might be used to make saucepans?

From anglers to aeroplanes

Use the table opposite to help you answer these questions. In each case make sure you give a reason for your answer.

3 Which metals would be good for making electrical cables?

4 Which metal did anglers often use to weight their lines?

5 Which metal might be best for making aeroplane bodies?

MADE WITH METAL

The pictures on this page illustrate some of the many ways that metals have been used, both recently and in the past.

Copper is quite a soft metal, so these pipes are quite easily bent into shape. They are joined with **brass** fittings.

This **aluminium** foil is used to wrap food for storage and cooking.

This **bronze** cat dates from 30 BC.

These knives are made from **stainless steel**.

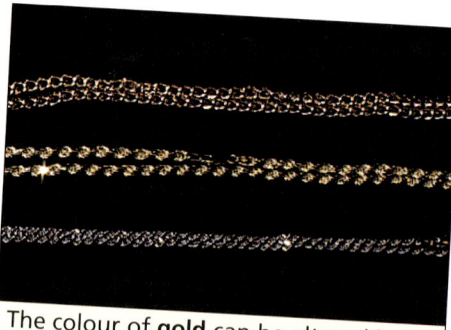

The colour of **gold** can be altered by mixing it with small amounts of **copper** (to make it redder) or **zinc** and **nickel** (to make it paler).

This Roman coin is made of **silver** …

… but these modern ones are made of **cupronickel**.

Before plastics were invented, **iron** coated with **zinc** was often used to make cans and buckets.

Thin sheets of **lead** can be folded to make flashing around a chimney to stop rainwater getting into the roof.

Alloys

This table gives information about some alloys. It will help you with the activities on this page.

Use a list of symbols for metals to help you write down the full name of each metallic element in this table.

Spot the alloy

1 Which of the metals shown in the pictures on the opposite page are pure metals? Which are alloys?

2 What is one advantage of using brass fittings, rather than copper, to join pipes?

3 Why is stainless steel better than mild steel for making knives?

4 Why is silver not used nowadays for making coins?

Alloy	Typical composition		Properties
Brass	Cu	60%	Golden appearance, malleable (bendy, easily worked), resistant to corrosion, harder than copper or zinc
	Zn	40%	
Cupronickel	Cu	70%	Silver appearance, other properties as brass
	Ni	30%	
Duralumin	Al	95%	Low density, stronger and more corrosion resistant than aluminium
	Cu	3%	
	Mg	1%	
	Mn	1%	
Bronze	Cu	90%	Golden appearance, resistant to corrosion, hard-wearing
	Sn	10%	
Mild steel	Fe	99.8%	Strong yet malleable (easily worked)
	C	0.2%	
High-strength steel	Fe	96%	Very high strength even when hot
	W	3%	
	C	1%	
Stainless steel	Fe	74%	Harder than mild steel, very resistant to corrosion, shiny
	Cr	18%	
	Ni	8%	
Alnico	Fe	35%	Good magnetic properties
	Co	30%	
	Ni	25%	
	Al	10%	

Which alloy and why?

Alloying is sometimes used to change the appearance of a metal, but that is often not the main reason for using an alloy.

Write down as many reasons as you can for making pure metals into alloys.

5 Which alloy do you think would be best for making the following? Give reasons in each case:

- kitchen sinks
- surgical instruments
- bits for high-speed drills
- magnets
- car bodies
- aeroplane wings

Metals then and now

Use library books to find out roughly the dates when bronze, brass, iron, steel and aluminium were first used. Use what you find out to draw a time line showing 'Metals through the ages'.

Use pictures from magazines and leaflets to make a poster showing some uses of metals. Give your poster a title.

WHERE DO METALS COME FROM?

Ores

An **ore** is a rock containing minerals that can be treated to produce a metal. Some ores contain pure metal, but more often the metal is part of a compound, so getting the metal from an ore nearly always involves a chemical reaction.

Lead ore used to be mined and treated in the Yorkshire Dales.

These pictures show some metal ores. The name of the ore and the symbol for the mineral in it are given beneath the pictures.

This is a copper ore mine in Queensland, Australia.

Lead ore
Galena (PbS)

Copper is sometimes found as the metal (Cu) but is more often combined with other elements.

Potassium
Sodium
Lithium
Calcium
Magnesium
Aluminium
Zinc
Iron
Lead
Copper
Silver
Gold
Platinum

More about ores

Galena (PbS) is a compound of lead and sulphur. Its chemical name is lead sulphide. The chemical name for bauxite is aluminium oxide. Its chemical formula, Al_2O_3, tells us that it has two aluminium atoms for every three oxygen atoms.

Zinc ore
Sphalerite (ZnS)

1 What is the chemical name for sphalerite?

◀ *This table lists some metals in order of their reactivity, with the most reactive at the top.*

2 Which metals are found uncombined? Where are they in the table of reactivity?

3 Which other metal in the table might you expect to find uncombined?

4 Which metals do you think are likely to be the most difficult to extract from their ores?

Gold ore
Quartz with uncombined gold (Au)

Tin ore
Cassiterite (SnO_2)

Aluminium ore
Bauxite (Al_2O_3)

Silver ore
Uncombined silver (Ag)

Mixtures of compounds

When a metal is combined with other elements, the metal itself makes up only part of the overall mass of the compound. For example, about 1.2 tonnes of **pure** *lead sulphide (PbS) are needed to make 1 tonne of lead, and about 2 tonnes of* **pure** *aluminium oxide (Al_2O_3) are needed to make 1 tonne of aluminium.*

In most ores, the compound containing the metal is itself mixed with other materials, so the metal itself makes up an even smaller proportion of the overall mass. The table below shows how much ore is typically needed to make 1 tonne of some metals.

Chalcopyrite and bornite are both compounds of copper, iron and sulphur.

Malachite is a compound of copper, carbon, oxygen and hydrogen.

Haematite, magnetite and goethite are all iron ores. They are all compounds of iron and oxygen.

Look at the table and discuss the following questions.

- Of the examples listed in the table, which ore contains the greatest amount of unwanted material? Why is it worthwhile to mine this ore?

- Why is it worth mining rocks that contain only fairly small amounts of copper, while iron ores are used only if they contain quite a large proportion of iron?

- Aluminium and iron compounds are both quite common in rocks that lie near the surface of the earth, and the ores that are mined contain a large proportion of metal for both aluminium and iron. However, aluminium metal is over 10 times more expensive than iron. Why do you think this might be?

Metal	Typical mass of ore needed to make 1 t of pure metal
Aluminium	3 t
Copper	50 t
Gold	1 000 000 t
Iron	2 t
Lead	16 t

FROM ORE TO METAL

Some metals can be extracted from their ores by heating the ore in a furnace with coke. This process is called **smelting**. Other metals are more difficult to extract because they are more reactive.

Smelting iron

*Iron is smelted from its ore (iron oxide) in a **blast furnace**.*

Iron ore …

… coke…

… and limestone …

Blast furnaces are typically over 60 m high. They run continuously because it wastes a lot of energy if they cool and have to be heated up again.

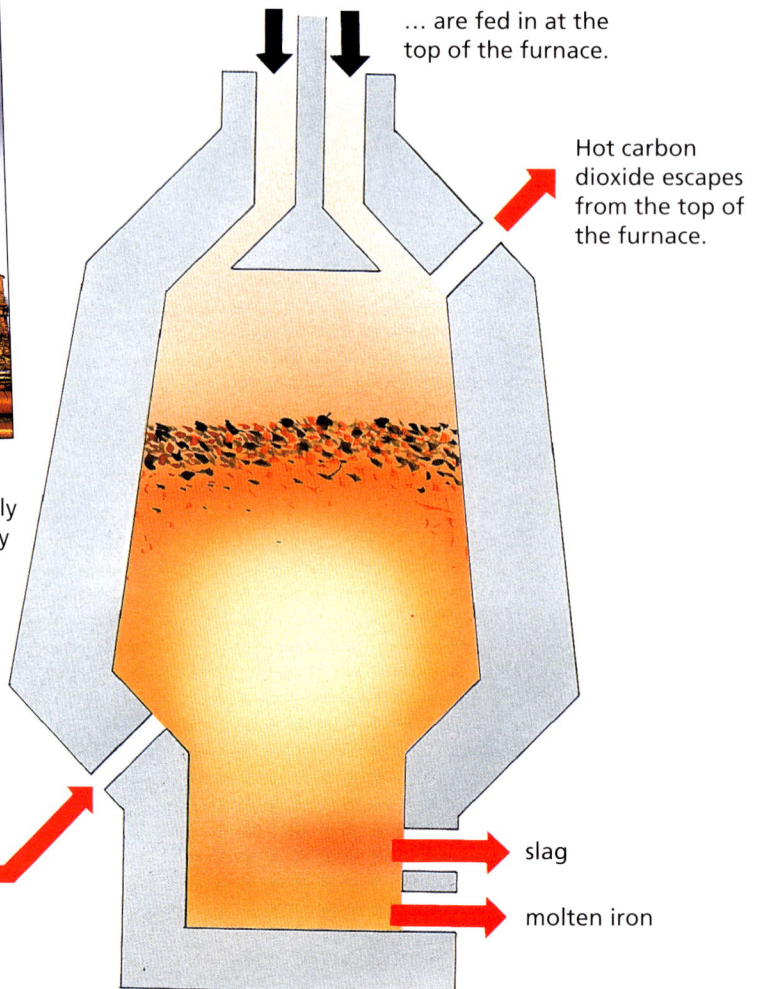

… are fed in at the top of the furnace.

Hot carbon dioxide escapes from the top of the furnace.

Hot air is blown in to make the coke burn fiercely.

slag

molten iron

70

Inside the furnace

Carbon from the coke and oxygen from the air combine to form a gas called carbon monoxide:

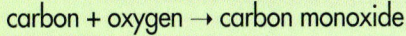

carbon + oxygen → carbon monoxide

The carbon monoxide reacts with the iron oxide ore to form iron. Carbon dioxide gas is also produced.

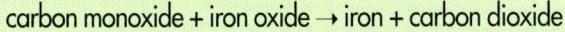

carbon monoxide + iron oxide → iron + carbon dioxide

The iron oxide is reduced and the carbon monoxide is oxidized.

1 Why do you think the furnace is called a blast furnace?

2 Look carefully at a piece of coke. Why do you think it makes an ideal fuel for a blast furnace?

Molten iron is run off at the bottom of a blast furnace and slag forms slightly higher up.

Limestone cleans up

The limestone is used to remove sand and other earthy materials that might clog up the furnace. Sand reacts with limestone to make a glassy substance called **slag**.
The molten slag and molten iron trickle down to the bottom of the furnace.
The slag floats on top of the iron so it can be taken out separately.

What happens next?

The iron from a blast furnace may be cooled to form blocks. It needs further treatment before it can be used.

3 Iron from a blast furnace contains up to 5% carbon. Where do you think this comes from?

4 What kinds of treatment do you think iron might go through before it is used?

The iron that comes out of the blast furnace is called pig iron.

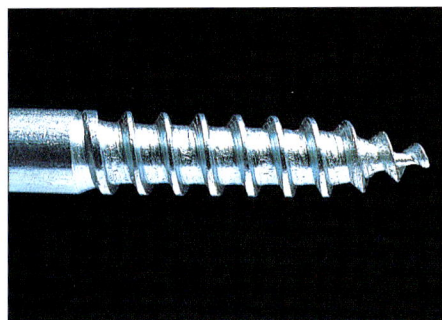

Iron is treated before being used to make bridges or screws.

ELEMENTS ALL TOGETHER

Families

This chart is called the **Periodic Table** of the elements. It lists all the elements. Each row of the table is called a **period**, and each column is called a **group**. Each group is a family of elements that have many things in common.

									Groups										
		I	II											III	IV	V	VI	VII	VIII
1								H Hydrogen											He Helium
2		Li Lithium	Be Beryllium											B Boron	C Carbon	N Nitrogen	O Oxygen	F Fluorine	Ne Neon
3		Na Sodium	Mg Magnesium											Al Aluminium	Si Silicon	P Phosphorus	S Sulphur	Cl Chlorine	Ar Argon
4		K Potassium	Ca Calcium	Sc Scandium	Ti Titanium	V Vanadium	Cr Chromium	Mn Manganese	Fe Iron	Co Cobalt	Ni Nickel	Cu Copper	Zn Zinc	Ga Gallium	Ge Germanium	As Arsenic	Se Selenium	Br Bromine	Kr Krypton
5		Rb Rubidium	Sr Strontium	Y Yttrium	Zr Zirconium	Nb Niobium	Mo Molybdenum	Tc Technetium	Ru Ruthenium	Rh Rhodium	Pd Palladium	Ag Silver	Cd Cadmium	In Indium	Sn Tin	Sb Antimony	Te Tellurium	I Iodine	Xe Xenon
6		Cs Caesium	Ba Barium	La Lanthanum	Hf Hafnium	Ta Tantalum	W Tungsten	Re Rhenium	Os Osmium	Ir Iridium	Pt Platinum	Au Gold	Hg Mercury	Tl Thallium	Pb Lead	Bi Bismuth	Po Polonium	At Astatine	Rn Radon
7		Fr Francium	Ra Radium	Ac Actinium															

Periods (vertical label)

Ce Cerium	Pr Praseodymium	Nd Neodymium	Pm Promethium	Sm Samarium	Eu Europium	Gd Gadolinium	Tb Terbium	Dy Dysprosium	Ho Holmium	Er Erbium	Tm Thulium	Yb Ytterbium	Lu Lutetium
Th Thorium	Pa Protactinium	U Uranium	Np Neptunium	Pu Plutonium	Am Americium	Cm Curium	Bk Berkelium	Cf Californium	Es Einsteinium	Fm Fermium	Md Mendelevium	No Nobelium	Lr Lawrencium

☐ = metals

☐ = non-metals

Group I

The elements in this group are all metals that react violently with water, sometimes catching fire as they react.

Potassium is more reactive than sodium, and sodium is more reactive than lithium.

1 How would you expect the reactivity of caesium to compare with that of potassium?

These elements all react readily with non-metallic elements to produce compounds (such as oxides and chlorides). The compounds are all white, and dissolve easily in water to give colourless solutions.

Sodium reacting with water

Potassium reacting with water

Group VII

*This group of elements is called the **halogens**. They are all non-metals. They all make coloured, choking fumes.*

2 Would you expect astatine to be a solid, a liquid or a gas at room temperature?

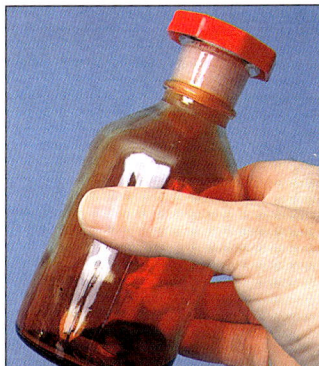
Bromine is a liquid that produces a brown vapour at room temperature.

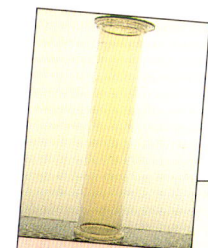
Fluorine and chlorine are gases at room temperature.

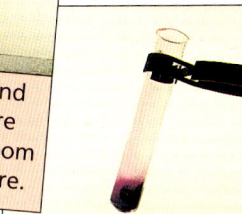
Iodine is a solid that produces a purple vapour when warmed gently.

Group VIII

*This group is called the **noble gases**. Together, they make up about 1% of the air. They are very unreactive.*

Helium is used to fill balloons and airships because its density is very low. It does not burn so there is no danger of its catching fire.

Argon is used to fill light bulbs. It stops the metal filament from burning up.

Friends and neighbours

As well as the groups being 'families', other elements that are close to each other in the Periodic Table have things in common. For example, the non-metallic elements are on the right of the table.

The only elements that are gases are hydrogen, nitrogen, oxygen, fluorine, chlorine and the noble gases.

3 Whereabouts in the table are the gases found?

Each of the following sets of 'friends' has something in common.

Find them in the Periodic Table.

● Iron, cobalt and nickel are the only three elements that are strongly magnetic.

● Silver, gold and platinum are unreactive metals that are used to make jewellery.

● Chromium, manganese, iron, cobalt and copper form many compounds that are coloured.

● Cadmium, mercury and lead are all dense, poisonous metals.

4 Which other metal might you expect to be poisonous?

● Thorium, protactinium, neptunium and plutonium are all radioactive.

5 Which other elements might you expect to be radioactive?

CURRENT THINKING

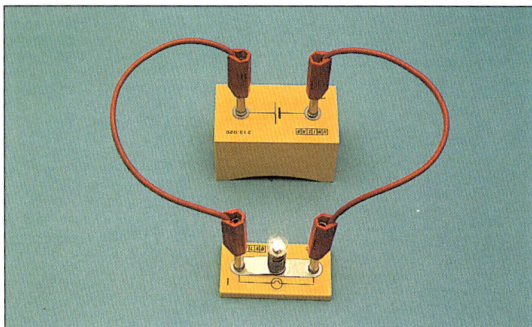

Try to describe how *you* think the current is behaving at different places in this circuit. Draw arrows and write labels on a circuit diagram like this one to show your ideas. ▶

Discuss your ideas with other students.

Current ideas

*In this circuit, the battery is producing an electric current and lighting the bulb. We cannot **see** what is happening inside the circuit, so we have to try to picture what is going on. The activities on this page will help you do this, and help you understand what happens.*

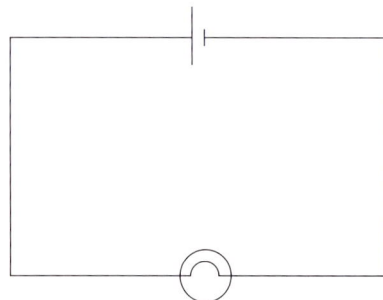

*If an idea is **correct**, it will be able to explain what happens in other circuits.*

1 Does your idea work for other circuits?

2 Are there any ideas that *cannot* explain what happens in this circuit?

*Another way to decide whether an idea is correct is to use it to **predict** the results of an experiment, and then find out whether the prediction is correct.*

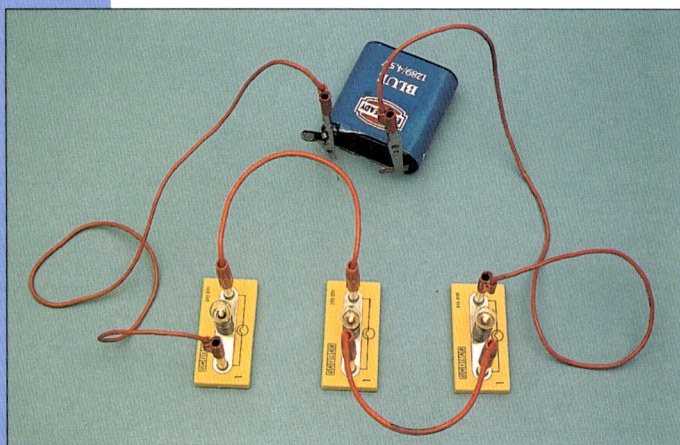

Use *one* idea about electric current to *predict* the result of measuring current at different places in a circuit. Write down your predictions.

What do scientists think?

Scientists think that an electric current is really millions of tiny particles, called **electrons**, flowing round the circuit. The battery gives the electrons energy. Electrons transfer energy to the lamp as they move through it. Most of the energy heats the filament, and some is given out as light. The electrons keep flowing at the same rate all round the circuit.

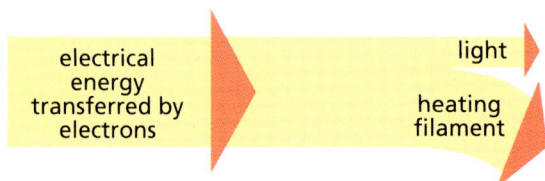

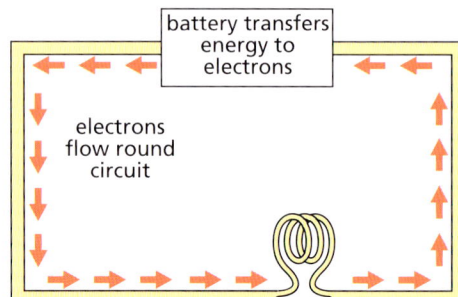

electrical energy transferred by electrons

light

heating filament

Current models

*You cannot **see** electrons, even with a microscope. So it can sometimes be helpful to picture different situations which are a bit like an electric current flowing in a circuit.*

Read about the three situations below. For each one, say what is behaving like:

- the electrons
- a lamp
- the battery
- the energy that is being transferred.

A simple heating system

The boiler heats the water, which then flows along the pipes and through the radiators. The water transfers energy from the boiler. In the radiators, energy from the water heats up the room. The water cannot escape, and no extra water can get in.

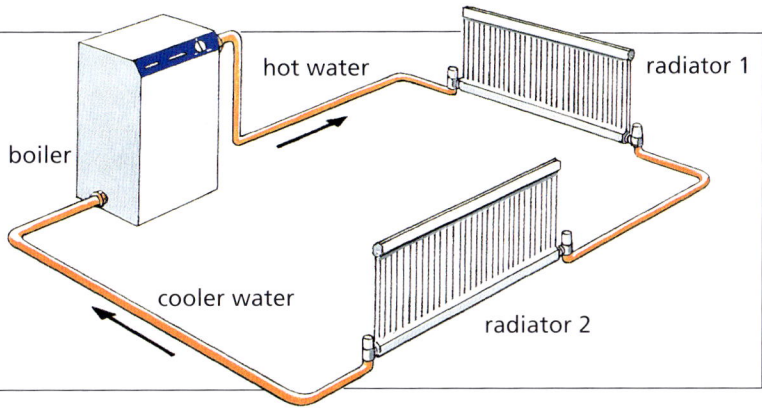

hot water

radiator 1

boiler

cooler water

radiator 2

A musical box

In this musical box, the belt is moved at a steady speed by the person turning the handle. The teeth on the belt pluck the metal strips to make different notes sound. The faster the handle is turned, the more sound is produced in a given time.

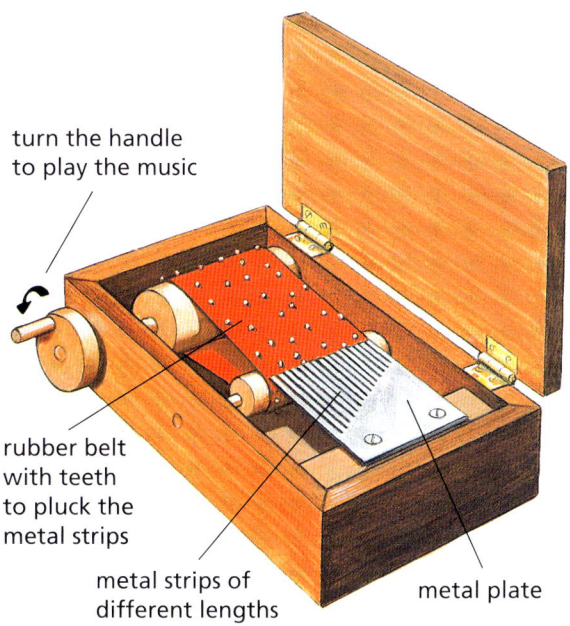

turn the handle
to play the music

rubber belt
with teeth
to pluck the
metal strips

metal strips of
different lengths

metal plate

Running a marathon

Runners do several loops of the same circuit. Each time they pass the start, they grab a quick glucose drink. As they run, they gradually get tired. By the time they pass the start, they need another glucose drink to 'top up their energy'. No new runners join the race, none drop out – and they keep running at the same speed!

Decide which picture best helps *you* to understand electric current, and try to remember it. But remember that it is only *a bit like* a real circuit – it cannot tell you *everything* about how real circuits behave.

WHAT HAPPENS ...

This power station burns coal to power its generators. Power stations that burn other fuels (gas or oil, for example) work in the same way.

... IN A POWER STATION?

Questions of power

The following information describes stages in generating electricity.

Try to identify from the photograph the place where each stage is taking place.

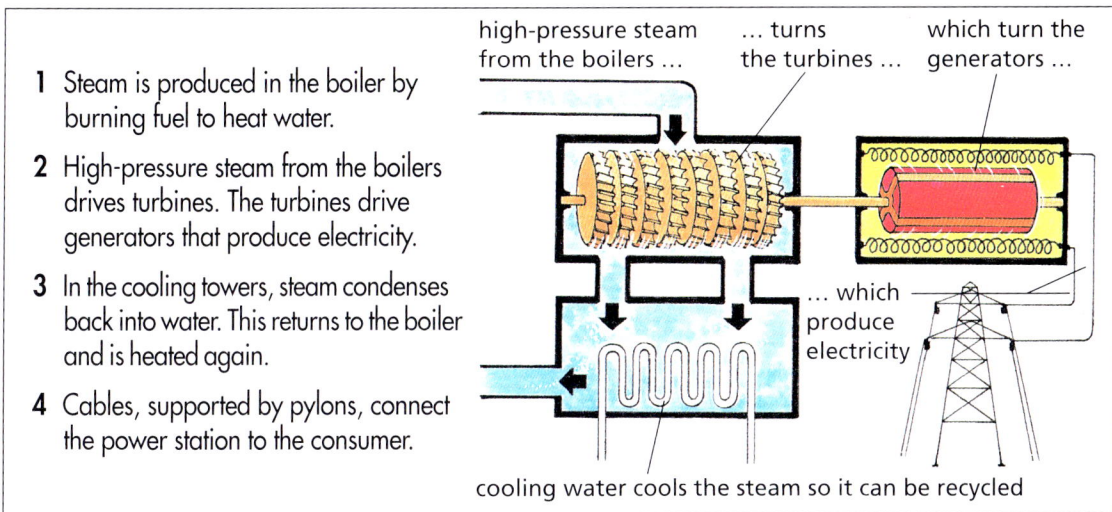

1 Steam is produced in the boiler by burning fuel to heat water.

2 High-pressure steam from the boilers drives turbines. The turbines drive generators that produce electricity.

3 In the cooling towers, steam condenses back into water. This returns to the boiler and is heated again.

4 Cables, supported by pylons, connect the power station to the consumer.

high-pressure steam from the boilers ...   ... turns the turbines ...   which turn the generators ...

... which produce electricity

cooling water cools the steam so it can be recycled

Suggest why power stations like the one in the picture are often built next to a river (there may be more than one reason).

1 The bills sent out by the electricity companies have to cover the cost of the fuel. What else do you think has to be paid for by the people who use electricity?

Energy transfer in a power station

This diagram summarizes the energy transferred by the power station.

energy stored in fuel

electrical energy

energy wasted in heating

Less than half the energy from the fuel is transferred as electrical energy. The rest is wasted.

Identify at least two places in the power station where energy is being wasted.

SPARKS AND FLASHES

When electrons move quickly through a gas
they can make it glow. All the pictures on
these two pages involve electrons moving
through a gas.

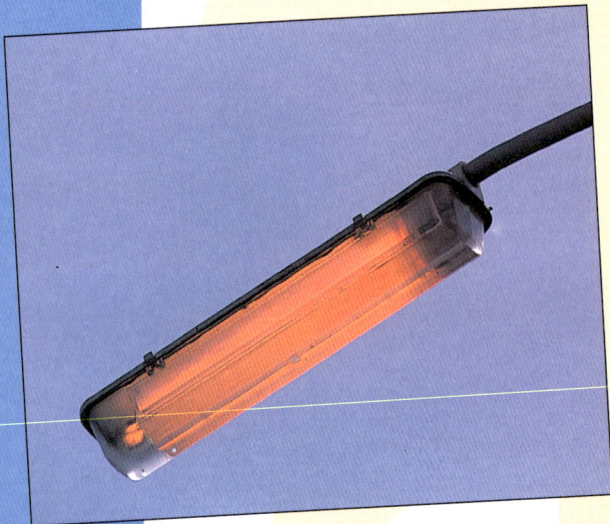

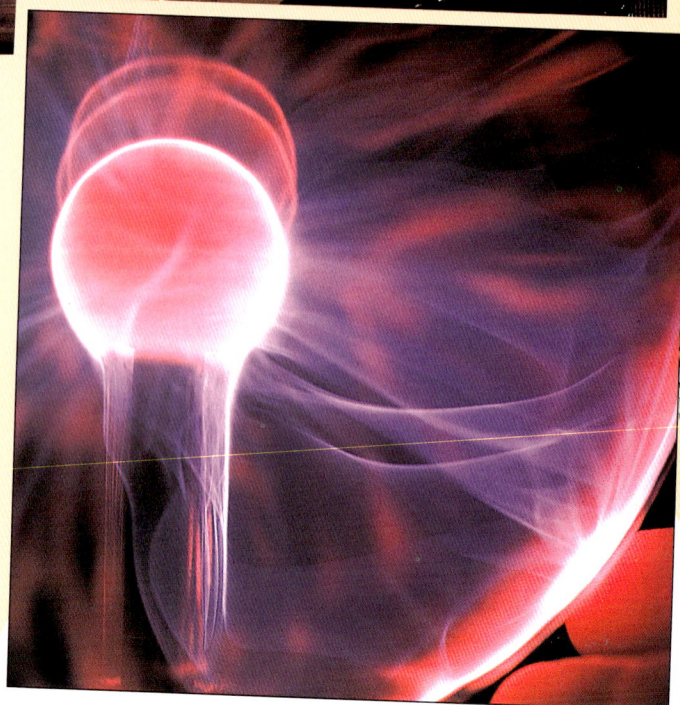

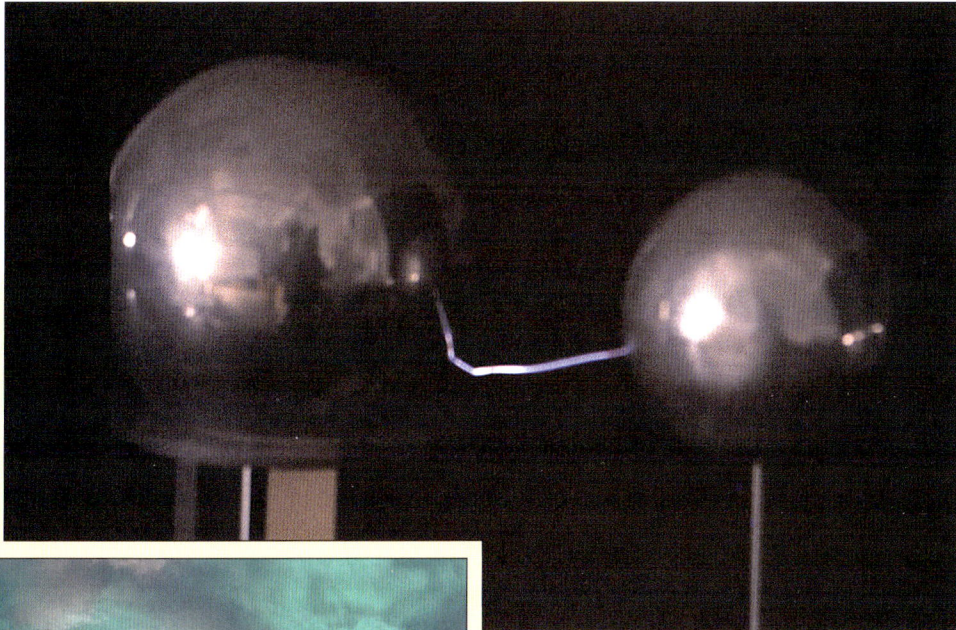

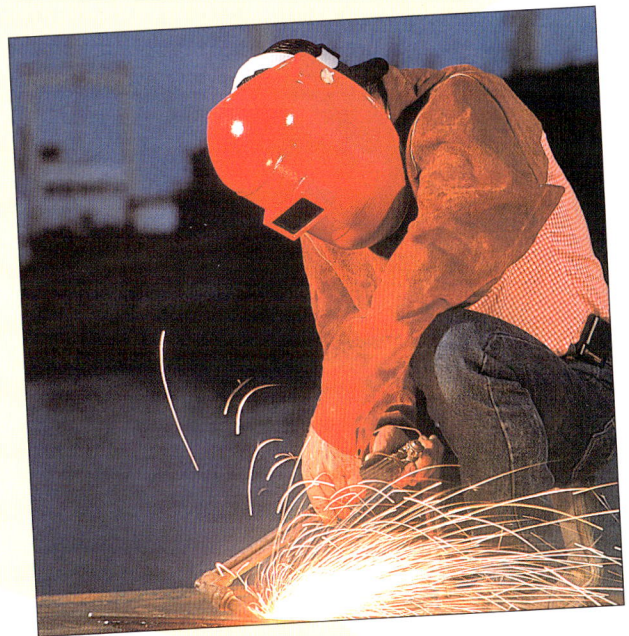

Discuss what you think is happening in each picture. Try to answer these questions.

- Are the electrons being made to move by a power supply or as a result of electrostatic charging?

- Is the electrons' movement controlled or accidental?

- Does the electrons' movement arise from natural events or are people causing it?

FOG IN NOVEMBER

Veena and Sujata were reading
TV This Week and noticed a new
television programme about science and
the environment.

7.30 World Watch

> **NEW** First in a series linking scientific
> ideas to stories about the world around us.
>
> **Fog in November**
>
> The poor air quality experienced last
> year when a blanket of fog lay over Britain
> raises certain questions. What causes fog?
> Why does the air quality fall in foggy
> weather? Where does the pollution come
> from, and where does it go?
> World Watch investigates.

Some scenes from the first **'World Watch'**
programme are shown on these two pages.

For over a week during last November, central
England lay under a blanket of fog.

… and why do cars pour out the nitrogen oxides
that help produce the fog, as well as pollute the air?

Is the only way to improve the environment to do
without electricity, or cars?

This British pollution causes acid rain in Norway and
Sweden, damaging trees and lakes there.

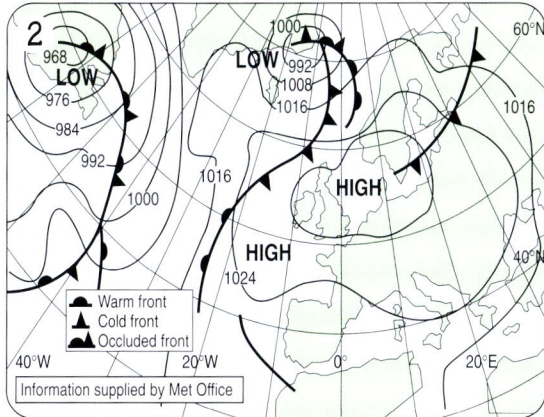

A high-pressure air mass brought cold, calm conditions which prevented air pollutants being carried away.

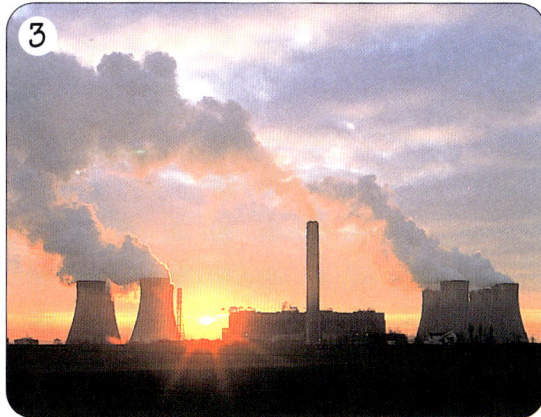

'World Watch' decided to investigate the possible sources of pollution. How much harmful sulphur dioxide do coal-burning power stations produce ...

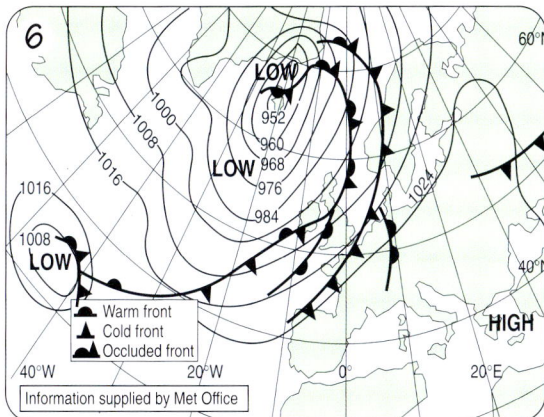

Eventually, weather conditions returned to normal as the high-pressure air mass was replaced by a south-westerly airstream ...

... bringing wet, windy weather to Britain, and carrying the polluted air to Scandinavia.

10 Should we in Britain pay? Or should we try to reduce the amount of air pollution we produce daily, but which does not seem to affect us except at times like last November?

One solution is to add limestone to affected Scandinavian lakes and rivers to neutralize the acidity.

Points of view

Use this unit to find out more about:

- air masses and weather
- the effects of acid rain
- ways of reducing air pollution.

Discuss how you would answer the final question posed in the television programme. Make notes of your ideas.

81

WORLD WATCHING

Our Features Editor talks to …
ANDREW BATTYE, producer of the new series *World Watch*.

Andrew Battye is a man with a mission. His series World Watch shows the crucial role of science in understanding the environment.

The story begins on 27 April 1986 when a fire broke out inside a nuclear reactor at Chernobyl.

'Caring about endangered species and recycling bottles is not enough,' said Andrew in an interview at his North London home. 'How can anyone have sensible opinions about environmental issues if they don't know how the world works?'

'Take the accident at Chernobyl in 1986, when there was an explosion and fire at a nuclear reactor. Most people knew that something harmful had been released, but had little idea of what it was or why it was dangerous.

'I wanted to make a different sort of documentary about the Chernobyl accident. I wanted to use the incident to help people understand more about radioactivity and ionizing radiation.'

What has a sheep sale in Cumbria to do with a nuclear accident that happened a thousand miles away, and several years ago?

Each of Andrew's *World Watch* programmes tells a story which makes links between science and the environment. *TV This Week* brings you a preview of Tuesday's programme.

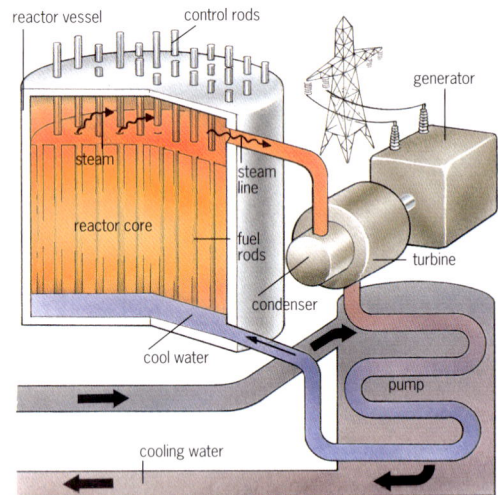

This type of reactor uses radioactive uranium fuel to boil water and create steam. The steam drives turbines which generate electricity.

'Although it's called a fuel, uranium doesn't actually burn,' explained Andrew. 'Its atoms are unstable and can be made to split into smaller atoms in a process called **nuclear fission**. The smaller atoms are very hot, so the reactor can heat water to form steam for the power station. Normally the reactor is kept from overheating by the water flowing around it. The fire at Chernobyl started because of a fault in the cooling system.

'As the reactor burned, clouds of smoke containing radioactive particles were released into the atmosphere. At that point, Chernobyl became an international problem because that smoke could blow wherever the wind took it.

'Substances that are radioactive emit small, electrically charged particles and high-energy radiation. Together these are known as **ionizing radiation**.

'Ionizing radiation is potentially dangerous because it can damage animal and plant cells. Close to Chernobyl, radiation levels were very high, and a number of people died from the effects soon after the accident. Any increase in radiation also increases the long-term risk of cancer.

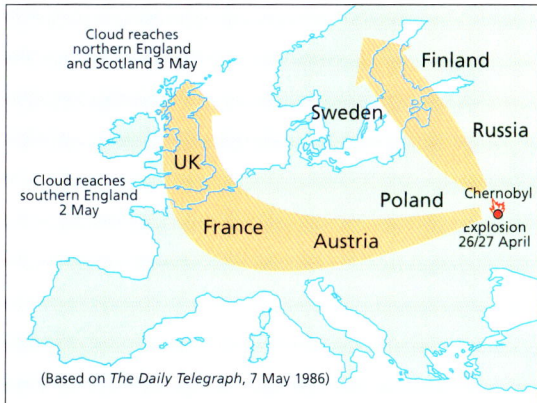

Cloud reaches northern England and Scotland 3 May

Finland

Sweden

Russia

UK

Cloud reaches southern England 2 May

France

Poland

Austria

Chernobyl

explosion 26/27 April

(Based on *The Daily Telegraph*, 7 May 1986)

At first, radioactive particles were blown north-eastwards over Scandinavia. Then the weather changed, and a cloud of radioactive particles was blown westwards towards Britain.

Lake District, Isle of Man, SW, NE, NW Scotland, Glasgow, Central Highlands, Moray Firth, Argyll, Northern Ireland: Rather cloudy, a little drizzle in places, but sunny intervals developing: wind S or SE light: max temp 17C (63F).

Outlook for tomorrow and Sunday: Generally similar, but outbreaks of thundery rain developing over England and Wales spreading to remaining districts.

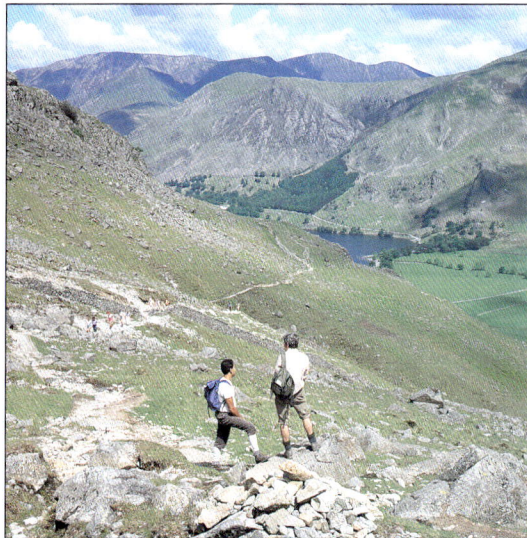

On 2 May, when the cloud arrived, showers were forecast for northern Britain. Where it rained, large numbers of radioactive particles fell to the ground. The level of ionizing radiation detected was much greater than normal.

Contour map of the Chernobyl fallout, in becquerels per square metre
(© *The Guardian*, 1986)

'What many people don't realize,' said Andrew, 'is that there is a certain amount of **background radiation** around us all the time. A proportion of all the atoms that make up the world are **decaying**, and emitting ionizing radiation. A nuclear power plant uses a concentrated source of radiation.

'The particles which fell from the Chernobyl cloud added to the background radiation which is normally present. They contaminated water supplies, and grass, and began to enter the food chain. Later, when they were washed down through the soil, they could be taken up by plants. Again, as sheep ate the grass, the radioactive substances entered the food chain. Some, like iodine, decay very quickly, but others, like caesium, are very persistent indeed.'

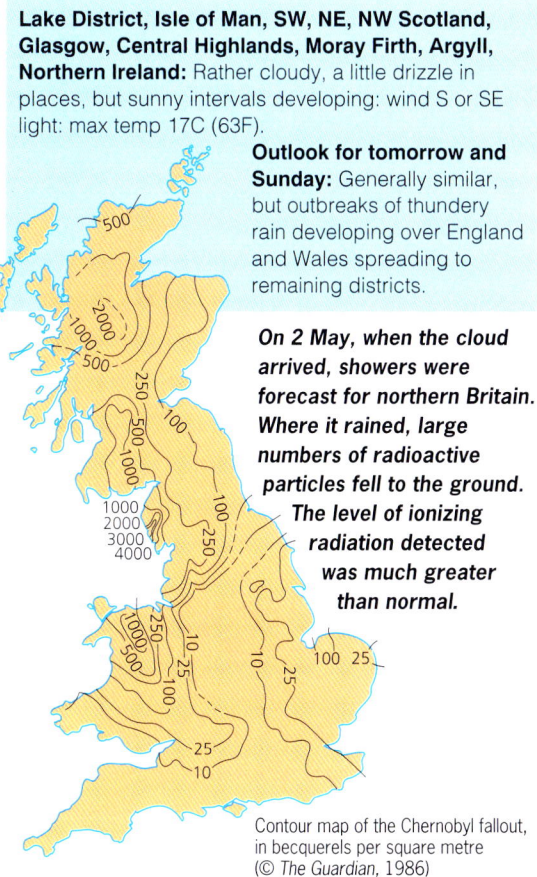

This grass in Cumbria is more radioactive than usual. The low dose of ionizing radiation does walkers little harm because the radioactive particles are outside their bodies.

However, this sheep eats grass, so radioactive particles will enter its body and continue to emit ionizing radiation for as long as they remain there.

Still puzzled about radioactivity and ionizing radiation? Then tune in to *World Watch*.

SALT OF THE EARTH

WORLD
WATCH

7.30

World Watch

The third programme in a series linking scientific ideas to stories about the world around us.

Salt of the earth

Salt is vital for life, and a useful starting material for many of the chemicals we need to maintain our lifestyle in the developed world. Where does salt come from, and how do salt deposits form?
World Watch unravels a story which begins with energy from the earth, and ends with energy from the sun.

Lake Magadi in Kenya is no ordinary lake. The dredger is scooping a mixture of solid salts – mainly sodium chloride and sodium carbonate.

Millions of years ago, red-hot lavas erupted from volcanos here. Now rain water seeps through the solid lava, dissolving salts as it does so.

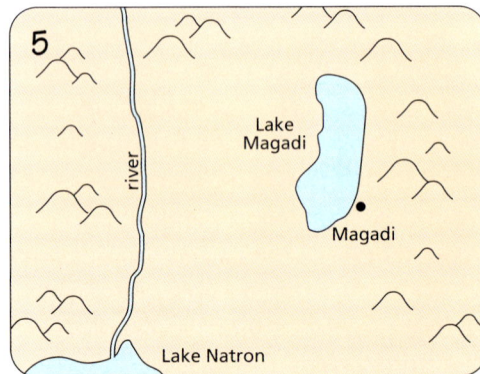

Lake Magadi is fed by salt water springs, but it has no outlet. In the heat of the sun, water evaporates from the lake, and the salt gets more and more concentrated.

Unlike the salts at Lake Magadi, this mine produces only sodium chloride. And unlike the deposit at Lake Magadi which is producing salt faster than the Kenyans can collect it, this one is being used up.

Like the Kenyans we use salt on our food, but we also spread large quantities of unpurified rock salt on the roads in winter.

The salt mixture is separated at this lakeside factory. Sodium chloride is used locally, but most of the sodium carbonate is exported for use in glass and soap manufacture.

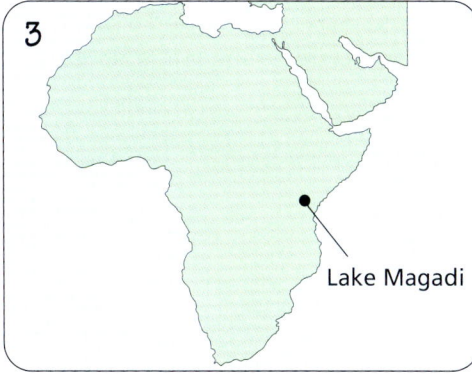

Why is Lake Magadi salty? The answer lies deep within the earth. Lake Magadi is in the Rift Valley region of Africa.

Deep below the ground in this Cheshire mine are salt deposits which formed over 200 million years ago.

At this time, the climate in Britain must have been similar to that of Kenya today. There were no humans – this was the age of the dinosaur.

All these products owe their existence to salt deposits that formed, and are still forming, because of energy from the earth which produces lavas, and energy from the sun which drives the water cycle.

Salt is also used to make sodium hydroxide and sodium carbonate. These alkalis formed the basis of the British chemical industry 100 years ago.

Find out more:

- about different salts
- about other salt deposits in the world
- about how alkalis are made from sodium chloride
- about why sodium chloride is spread on icy roads in winter.

THE CHANGING EARTH

Mei sent off for a 'World Watch' poster which was produced to accompany the last programme in the series, **Cycling Round the World**.

▢ Read the poster carefully.

▢ Make a list of all the different cycles described in the poster.

CYCLING ROUND THE WORLD

The world around us is changing constantly. The days, the seasons, the weather and the formation of the landscape are driven by processes which link together to form complex systems and cycles.

A *THE EARTH FROM SPACE*

B *A STORM FORCE GALE*

The spinning of the earth causes winds like the jet stream in the upper atmosphere. These, together with the heating of air masses by the sun, cause areas of high and low air pressure in the lower atmosphere. Winds blow from high- to low-pressure areas.

C *WAVES AND FLOODS*
Wind whips up waves on the sea. A high wind coupled with a high tide can lead to flooding at the coast. Tides are caused by the gravitational pull on the earth as it is circled by the moon.

D *A LANDSCAPE SHAPED BY WATER*
Water evaporates from sea and land, condenses to form rain and snow and flows back to the sea via streams and rivers. This water cycle is driven by the sun, and by gravity. Water and ice wear down the rocks to create a variety of landscapes.

The spinning of the earth on its own axis gives day and night, and the orbit of the earth around the sun gives the seasons. The satellite image shows swirls of cloud – water vapour in the atmosphere.

Find out as much as you can about each of the cycles.

For each cycle:

● draw a flow chart to describe what happens

● discuss how long you think each cycle takes to complete.

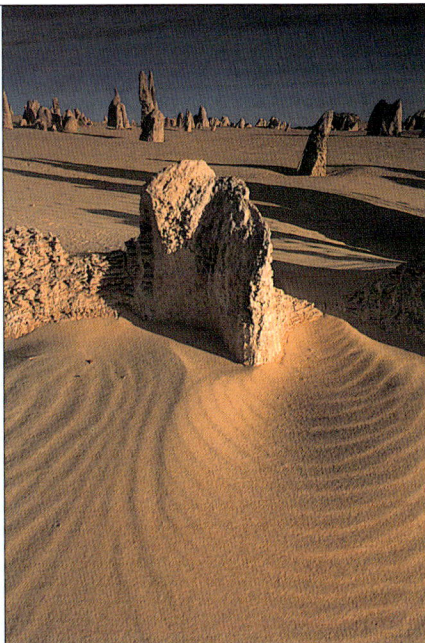

E *A LANDSCAPE SHAPED BY WIND*

In dry areas of the world, spectacular landscapes form as wind-blown particles scour the rocks or are deposited in dunes.

F *NEW ROCKS FROM THE DEEP*

The decay of radioactive elements deep within the earth causes heating. In some areas new rocks are formed as molten magma escapes to the surface. The lava flow which created Iceland is causing the Atlantic Ocean to widen and the continents on either side to move apart. In other places, the earth's crust is being carried downwards, deep into the earth. New igneous rocks are continually being created and destroyed.

G *THE LIVING WORLD*

Plants need water, warmth and a supply of minerals, weathered from the rocks. Directly or indirectly, plants depend on the sun for all of these things. They also need sunlight for photosynthesis – to turn water and carbon dioxide into sugar and starch. Herbivores eat plants; carnivores eat other animals. When plants and animals die, decomposer organisms break them down and the cycle of life begins again.

LOOKING TO THE FUTURE

First ideas

Andrew Battye is planning the next series of 'World Watch'. He thinks that the question of how best to generate electricity in the future would make an interesting programme. In the first stage of his research, Andrew has asked the picture library to send him photographs showing electricity generation using:

- fossil fuels
- nuclear fuels
- running water
- wind
- tides
- biomass
- waves
- hot rocks
- the sun.

Look at the photographs and decide which of these examples the picture researcher has been able to find for Andrew.

Use books and leaflets to find out more about each of the methods Andrew listed.

Thinking it through

In each of the methods of generating electricity, energy is being transferred from one form to another.

Draw energy arrow diagrams to show the energy transfers that take place in each one.

1 Which methods use renewable and which use non-renewable forms of energy?

Think of as many advantages and disadvantages as you can for each of the methods listed.

Discuss whether or not each method could be widely used in Britain.

Finding an angle

Suppose you were planning a programme about electricity generation. Would you choose to compare all the different methods, or concentrate on just one? From what angle would you tell your story – would you concentrate on explaining how electricity is generated, on pollution, or on the depletion of non-renewable sources of energy? Would you choose your local power station as an example, or an exotic foreign location? What factors would influence your choice of story?

Plan your own *World Watch* programme about electricity generation.

You might:

- use drawings or photographs cut from magazines to create a storyboard
- write a shooting script for the programme
- design an educational poster to accompany the progamme
- write an article or design advertising material to promote the programme.

Planning more programmes

Planning a science programme or article is a good way to revise the science you have learned.

Look through *Science Focus* and find other science topics that would make interesting *World Watch* programmes.

INDEX

Acknowledgements

The Salters' Team is indebted to many companies and institutions for their encouragement and financial assistance; in particular, to

BP
Heinemann Educational
ICI
The Salters' Institute of Industrial Chemistry
The Training, Enterprise and Education Directorate
The University of York

Heinemann Educational,
a division of Heinemann Educational Books Ltd.
Halley Court, Jordan Hill, Oxford OX2 8EJ

OXFORD LONDON EDINBURGH
MADRID ATHENS BOLOGNA PARIS
MELBOURNE SYDNEY AUCKLAND SINGAPORE
TOKYO IBADAN NAIROBI HARARE
GABORONE PORTSMOUTH NH (USA)

ISBN 0 435 63022 9

First published 1994

94 95 96 97 98 10 9 8 7 6 5 4 3 2 1

Designed and typeset by Ken Vail Graphic Design
Printed in Hong Kong

Photo Acknowledgements

The authors and publishers are grateful to the staff, students and parents of Northbrook CE School in Lee, Lewisham for their co-operation in producing many of the photographs which appear in this series. In particular, they would like to thank John Walters, John Hickman, Adam, Alan, Amelia, Bethlehem, Carol, Gary, Gavin, Kevin, Linda, Paul, Simone, Tina, Tracy and Zoe.

The authors and publishers are grateful to the following for permission to reproduce photographs:

p3 *TR, MT, MB* Holt Studios International/ Nigel Cattlin, *BL* Martin Bond/Science Photo Library, *BR* J Allan Cash;

p4 *L* Holt Studios International/Nigel Cattlin, *ML* Ron Giling/Panos Pictures, *MR* The Hutchison Library, *R* David Reed/Panos Pictures;

p6 *M* M I Walker/Science Photo Library, *B* Long Ashton Research Station;

p8 Philip Parkhouse;

p12 *TL* Zefa, *TR* Anatol/Zefa, *B* Robert Harding Picture Library;

p13 *T* Sally & Richard Greenhill, *B* Zefa;

p14 *T* Zefa-Damm, *ML* & *B* Sally & Richard Greenhill, *MR* Chris Vasiliou/Barnaby's Picture Library;

p15 Judith Ramsden;

p18 *T* Sheperd Design & Build, *B* The Coca-Cola Company;

p19 *T* Brian Gibbs/Barnaby's Picture Library, *M* J Allan Cash;

p24 *TL* Holt Studios International/Nigel Cattlin, *TR* John Lazonby, *BL* Courage Brewery, *BR* J Allan Cash;

p25 *TL* Moreland Brewery Abingdon, *TM* Courage Brewery, *TR* John Lazonby, *ML* Sally & Richard Greenhill;

p26 D Malin/Royal Observatory Edinburgh/ Planetarium Armagh;

p28 Phil Findlay;

p29 Chemistry Photographics, University of York;

p30 *L* NASA/Science Photo Library, *R* Planetarium Armagh;

p31 *L* Anglo-Australian Telescope Board/Planetarium Armagh, *R* JPL/IRAS, *B* MRAO, Cavendish Laboratory, Cambridge;

p32 Kobal Collection;

p33 *L* NASA/JPL/Planetarium Armagh, *TR* NASA/Science Photo Library, *ML* & *MR* NASA/JPL/ Planetarium Armagh;

p34 David Parker/Science Photo Library;

p35 *T* Royal Observatory Edinburgh/Planetarium Armagh, *ML* David Parker/Science Photo Library, *MR* Planetarium Armagh;

p36 Philip Parkhouse;

p38 *T* Barnaby's Picture Library;

p40 *TL* Dr Tony Brain/Science Photo Library, *TR* London School of Hygiene & Tropical Medicine/ Science Photo Library, *MR* Holt Studios International/Nigel Cattlin, *BL* J Allan Cash, *BM* Tony Craddock/Science Photo Library, *BR* Simon Fraser/Science Photo Library;

p41 *TR* Anthony Blake Photo Library, *B* Philip Parkhouse;

p42 *TR* & *BL* Zefa, ML Christopher Nicholson/Robert Harding Picture Library, *MR* Zefa/Hubrich, *BR* Zefa/Voigt;

p43 *TL* Zefa/Armstrong Roberts, *TR*, *MR* & *BR* Sally & Richard Greenhill;

p44 *TL* Colin Underhill/Barnaby's Picture Library, *TR* Zefa/Madison, *ML* Sally & Richard Greenhill, *BL* Zefa/Bond, *BR* David Cannon/Allsport;

p46 *T* J Allan Cash;

p49 *TM* Robert Harding Picture Library, *TR* J Allan Cash, *BL* & *BR* Sally & Richard Greenhill;

p50 Chris Priest & Mark Clarke/Science Photo Library;

p53 Sally & Richard Greenhill;

p58 Science Photo Library;

p59 *T* Sally & Richard Greenhill, *BL* & *BR* Biophoto Associates;

p62 *TL* Ronald Sheridan/Ancient Art & Architecture Collection, *TR* John P Stevens/Sheridan Photo Library/Ancient Art & Architecture Collection, *ML* & *B* J Allan Cash;

p63 *TL* Heini Schneebeli/Science Photo Library, *TR* J Allan Cash, *B* Barnaby's Picture Library;

p64 Physics Department, University of York;

p66 *TL, TM, ML, MM, BL* & *BR* Philip Parkhouse, *TR* Ronald Sheridan/Ancient Art & Architecture Collection, *MR* B Wilson/Sheridan Photo Library/Ancient Art & Architecture Collection, *BM* J Allan Cash;

p68 *TL* & *TR* J Allan Cash, *BR* Dr B Booth/GSF Picture Library, *others* Chemistry Photographics, University of York;

p69 *BMR* Dr B Booth/GSF Picture Library, *others* Chemistry Photographics, University of York;

p70 J Allan Cash;

p71 *TR* J Allan Cash, *MR* GSF Picture Library, *BL* Simon Fraser/Science Photo Library, *BR* Claude Nuridsany & Marie Perennou/Science Photo Library;

p72 Chemistry Photographics, University of York;

p73 *L* Chemistry Photographics, University of York, *TR* J Allan Cash, *BR* Philip Parkhouse;

p74 Chemistry Photographics, University of York;

p76 Robert Harding Picture Library;

p78 *T* Zefa, *BL* Robert Harding Picture Library, *BR* Alfred Pasieka/Science Photo Library;

p79 *T* Andrew Lambert, *ML* Keith Kent/Science Photo Library, *MR* Zefa, *B* John Walsh/Science Photo Library;

p80 *TR* Dr Harold Rose/Science Photo Library, *L* Sally & Richard Greenhill, *MR* Philip Parkhouse, *BR* Simon Fraser/Science Photo Library;

p81 *TR* Martin Bond/Science Photo Library, *MR* J Allan Cash, *B* Martin Bond/Environmental Picture Library;

p82 *BL* J Allan Cash, *TR* Novosti/Science Photo Library;

p83 *MR* J Allan Cash, *BR* Michael Durnan/Barnaby's Picture Library;

p84 *TR* Compix, *ML* Soames Summerhays/Science Photo Library, *BL* Salt Union Ltd, *BR* J Allan Cash;

p85 *TL* Compix, *ML* Salt Union Ltd, *MR* Ludek Pesek/Science Photo Library, *BL* Mansell Collection, *BR* Philip Parkhouse;

p86 *L* European Space Agency/Science Photo Library, *TR* & *BR* Robert Harding Picture Library;

p87 *TL* Paul Steel/Ace Photo Agency, *TR* Mats Wibe Lund/Sigurg. Jónasson, *BR* FHC Birch/Barnaby's Picture Library, *BR* Edmund Nagele/Ace Photo Agency;

p88 *A, B* & *C* Zefa, *D* Louis Salou/Robert Harding Picture Library, *E* Martin Bond/Science Photo Library, *F* Tony Waltham/Robert Harding Picture Library, *G* TJ Florian/Ace Photo Agency.

(*T* = top, *B* = bottom, *M* = middle, *L* = left, *R* = right)
All other photographs by Steve Smyth.

Acknowledgement is also due to the following for permission to reproduce copyright material:
p2, p83 © Times Newspapers Ltd 1991, 1986;
p83 © The Guardian.

While all reasonable efforts have been made to contact copyright holders, the publishers apologise to any copyright holder not acknowledged, and will correct any omissions brought to their attention.

Acknowledgement is made to Robin Seavill for original artwork on which some drawings are based.